MW01712067

# Things, Its and Aliens

Lobby Card Posters from Sci-fi Shockers!

A DENIS GIFFORD COLLECTION

BLOSSOM

An H. C. Blossom Book



ISBN 1 872532 58 6

Photography by Derek Smith and Jay Tauben

Design: Roger Lightfoot

Typeset in Great Britain by Uppercase

Printed and bound in Hong Kong

H. C. Blossom
6/7 Warren Mews
London W1P 5DJ

**Copyrights**

# Contents

*The selection of lobby cards is arranged in chronological order of the films' release dates.*

# *Looking at Lobby Cards*

Lobby Cards may be an unfamiliar term. It was to me when I started collecting them, many years ago. I was just a young film fan, picturegoer, cinema patron – there were several terms for the millions like us – and most of us collected some sort of memorabilia – an unknown term at the time. You know the kind of thing, the weekly fan magazines which, by the end of World War Two had reduced to just two, *Picturegoer* and *Picture Show* on alternate weeks. Then came a few tentative newcomers like *World Film Digest*, *Weekly Film News* and the start of a British edition of the pre-war American favourite, *Photoplay Monthly*. These were the popular collectables, the things everyone gradually built a pile of before handing them over to the local Boy Scouts' jumble sale. There were also the little monthly programmes, cardboard folders they gave out at the cinemas showing four weeks of double-bills and four weeks of Sunday reissues. These later were the great days for a film buff. Of course 'buff' was another word as yet unknown, except for its traditional British sense of stripped skin! The Sunday shows were something special, scratched old prints, stuck together with Sellotape, it seemed, by the number of snappings that suddenly brightened the screens with naked arclights. Nitrate prints on their last legs, going round just one more time for the benefit of us non-churchgoers interested in the history of films, and those cuddling courting couples who filled up the back rows, regardless of whether it was Boris Karloff or Mary Beth Hughes on the screen.

Then it was home to transpose those pencilled scribbles into my *Film Fan's Diary*, the start of a project that would, many years later, come to book publication as the *British Film Catalogue*. At the time, of course, British films were of much less interest to me than American films, just as the great Hollywood movies of a Golden Era seemed of considerably less interest than the latest adventures of the Bowery Boys, Ellery Queen or Boston Blackie. There was always something about a series, especially a B-bracket series, that attracted me far more than Jack Hulbert and Cicely Courtneidge, or Fred Astaire and Ginger Rogers. Even British series, few as they were, seemed more fun than James Mason and Margaret Lockwood at it again. Remember David Farrar as Sexton Blake?

But the really great fascination for me, and I suppose for millions of others, although I thought myself alone at the time, were the fantasy films. Horrors and science-fiction. The latter was thin on the screen before the boom began in the Fifties. As a boy before the war I had seen two SF films that had not only remained firmly imprinted in my memory, but had surely played a major part in moulding my interests. These were *The Invisible Man* and *Things to Come*, film masterworks by any standards, not just as fantasies. Both have classic lines I have always remembered. The first has an old farmer bursting in on a police conference with the words 'There's breathin' in me barn!', a line which is only outdone by the walrus-whiskered copper who watches wide-eyed as Claude Rains strips off his clothes revealing nothing. 'E's invisible, that's what's wrong with 'im!', says the bobby, dazed but unhazed. The spectacular H.G. Wells epic also has several. Raymond Massey, eyes fired with the future, speaks about the Rule of the Airmen, and at the end, as the first moon rocket is fired, everybody sings the closing question, 'Which Shall It Be?' Visually, of course, both films have equally classic moments, the footprints of the Invisible Man running in the snow, then falling as he is shot down by the police, and the breathtaking moment when the great bird-winged aircraft of the future come flying through the clouds – *Things to Come* indeed!

Unfortunately, perhaps, you'll find none of these moments reprinted here. It isn't that kind of book. Not that *The Invisible Man*, *Things to Come* and their wonderful ilk were not represented on lobby cards; they certainly were, but I haven't got them. Somebody, no doubt has somewhere, but probably not in Great Britain. Thanks to World War Two, old lobby cards were either handed over to Governmental waste paper drives – their thick texture must have made excellent cartridge cases – or the blank backs of them were used to overprint new lobby cards for new films. In time they disappeared altogether, their colourful images to be replaced by dull, grey monochrome stills, lacking in definition, smaller in size (ten by eight inches instead of fourteen by eleven), but who cared in the blackout?

Lobby cards came back to the cinemas, of course, in the Fifties, when the age of austerity was past and we were looking forward to the second half of the century. But even so, they were still designed, produced and printed in America, and dollars were not always available for such frivolities. That is why these wonderful souvenirs of yesterday's double-bills are so scarce on the ground in this country, and are seldom to be found, even at movie memorabilia fairs.

Lobby cards are made up in sets of eight, seven

scene stills and a title card. It is the title cards, of course, which are the most evocative and collectable, and frequently a mad collector will fork out a fortune for a full set, just to get his hands on a classic title card. I've done it myself! Some of them are in this book. Others you will find in the companion volume, *Mad Doctors, Monsters and Mummies.* And perhaps one day we will go beyond the mad end of the cinema spectrum and bring you a selection of westerns, or detectives, or comedies. But one thing is certain, most of them will be B-movies.

Incidentally, you may like to know that a selection of thirty of these science fiction lobby cards has been made up into a special book of postcards entitled *Things, Its and Aliens! Lobby Card Postcards from Sci-Fi Shockers!* Detach them along the perforated lines and send them to your friends!

*Denis Gifford*

THRILLS COME ROCKETING TO THE SCREEN
AS SCIENCE SMASHES
A NEW FRONTIER!
PROJECT
MOONBASE
They found romance 100,000 miles from the earth!
Terror strikes in the Unknown Stratosphere!
See man-piloted rocket launched from gigantic space ship!
with ROSS FORD · DONNA MARTELL · HAYDEN RORKE
Produced by JACK SEAMAN · Directed by RICHARD TALMADGE · Story and Screenplay by ROBERT HEINLEIN and JACK SEAMAN
A GALAXY PICTURES, INC. PRODUCTION · A Lippert Pictures Presentation

# Project Moonbase

*1953* Galaxy Pictures
*Distributor* Lippert Pictures
*Producer* Jack Seaman
*Associate Producer* Karl Johnson
*Director* Richard Talmadge
*Story* Robert A. Heinlein
*Screenplay* Robert A. Heinlein, Jack Seaman
*Camera* William Thompson
*Special Effects* Jacques Fresco
*Art Director* Jerome Pycha Jr
*Editor* Roland Gross
*Music* Herschel Burke Gilbert
63 minutes

Ross Ford *Major Moore*
Donna Martell *Colonel Briteis*
Hayden Rorke *General Greene*
Larry Johns *Dr Wernher*
Herb Jacobs *Dr Roundtree*
Barbara Morrison *Polly Prattles*
Ernestine Barrier *Madame President*
James Craven *Commodore Carlson*
John Hedloe *Adjutant*
Peter Adams *Capt Carmody*
Robert Karnes *Sam*
John Straub *Chaplain*
Charles Keane *Spacecom Operator*

'Thrills Come Rocketing to the Screen as Science Smashes a New Frontier!' screamed the publicity department via the lobby cards. *Variety*, the influential weekly review for the trade, thought differently: 'A ridiculous offering which even juve audiences won't accept'. Actually, it was a rather different screen the thrills were originally to come rocketing to – this movie is made up of a couple of episodes of a sci-fi series made for television, and children's television at that. However, what television rejects today, the cinema audiences will have thrust upon them tomorrow. Set in the then faraway future of 1970, a United States Space Force survey ship is sent to fly round the moon to check into the possibilities of setting up a base there. Captained by the aptly named Colonel Briteis, played by Donna Martell ('A cute little trick,' comments *Variety*), the ship makes a forced landing, thanks to a spy aboard. This is one Doctor Wernher, who is exposed as an imposter when he fails to know anything about the Brooklyn Dodgers! The result, 'They Found Romance a Hundred Thousand Miles from Earth!' Briteis and her handsome pilot, Major Moore, get married via a smiling chaplain and satellite television. Directed by silent screen stunt star Richard Talmadge, and scripted by, of all people, Robert *(Destination Moon)* Heinlein.

COSMIC FRANKENSTEIN TERRORIZES EARTH!
Already one whole city has been devoured...and still it grows, minute by minute, reaching out with countless invisible mouths to swallow the earth!
THE MAGNETIC MONSTER
The astounding story of the "thing" that came alive!
IVAN TORS presents
"THE MAGNETIC MONSTER" starring RICHARD CARLSON
featuring King Donovan · Jean Byron · Jarma Lewis · Screenplay by Curt Siodmak and Ivan Tors · Produced by IVAN TORS · Directed by CURT SIODMAK · An A-Men Production · Released thru United Artists
1

# The Magnetic Monster

*1953* A-Men Productions
*Distributor* United Artists
*Producer* Ivan Tors
*Director* Curt Siodmak
*Story* Curt Siodmak
*Screenplay* Curt Siodmak, Ivan Tors
*Camera* Charles Van Enger
*Special Effects* Harry Redmond Jr
*Art Director* George Van Marter
*Editor* Herbert L. Strock
*Music* Blaine Sanford
75 minutes

Richard Carlson *Jeffrey Stewart*
King Donovan *Dan Forbes*
Jean Byron *Connie Stewart*
Jarma Lewis *Stewardess*
Harry Ellerbe *Dr Allard*
Leo Britt *Dr Benton*
Leonard Mudie *Howard Denker*
Byron Foulger *Mr Simon*
Michael Fox *Dr Serny*
John Zaremba *Chief Watson*
Frank Gerstle *Colonel Willis*
John Vosper *Capt Dyer*
Billy Benedict *Albert*
Kathleen Freeman *Nellie*
Watson Downs *Mayor*
John Dodsworth *Cartwright*
Strother Martin *Co-pilot*

'Cosmic Frankenstein Terrorizes Earth!' – another good reason for Mary Wollstonecraft Shelley to sue, perhaps? Not really; this film is not half bad, thanks to a sincere script by sci-fi veteran Curt Siodmak, who also directed it. Richard Carlson, a fair actor in his way, plays the keen young married member of the OSI, which stands for the Office of Scientific Investigation. His partner, King Donovan, notices that the local Los Angeles air is getting radioactive. Then a lawn-mower runs wild in a hardware store, and soon magnetism is deduced. In no time the partners track the cause down to a dying scientist, old Leonard Mudie, who has discovered a new element, serranium, bombarded it with alpha particles for 200 hours, and changed it into an unstable, unipolar magnetic source that absorbs energy, turning it into matter so that it doubles its size every eleven hours, on the dot. Before the stuff can overrun the Earth, Carlson and Donovan hustle it off to Nova Scotia where they nullify the isotope with a charge of 900 million volts, precisely. Great sci-fi stuff, but all the fabulous special effects were clipped from an old 1934 German film entitled *Gold*.

HIS SECRET POWER MENACED THE WORLD!
He came from a billion miles of space to meet the strangest destiny ever told!
PHANTOM
FROM SPACE
1
"PHANTOM FROM SPACE"
Produced and Directed by W. Lee Wilder
Screenplay by Bill Raynor and Myles Wilder
Released Thru United Artists

# Phantom from Space

*1953* Planet Filmways
*Distributor* United Artists
*Producer* W. Lee Wilder
*Director* W. Lee Wilder
*Screenplay* Bill Raynor, Myles Wilder
*Camera* William Clothier
*Special Effects* Alex Welder, Howard Anderson
*Editor* George Gale
*Music* William Lava
72 minutes

Ted Cooper *Lt Hazen*
Rudolph Anders *Dr Wyatt*
Noreen Nash *Barbara Randall*
James Seay *Major Andrews*
Harry Landers *Lt Bowers*
Jack Daly *Wakeman*
Dick Sands *Phantom*
James Bannon
Michael Mark
Lela Nelson

The lobby cards billed nobody at all in this cut-price space caper, produced and directed by W. Lee Wilder, Billy Wilder's less-than-famous brother, and scripted by Myles Wilder, W. Lee Wilder's even less-than-famous son. A pity, really, as the cast included that harmonious pair, Rudolph Anders and Harry Landers. Before the credit titles even begin to appear, radar stations in Alaska are tracking an Unidentified Flying Object heading south at 5000 miles an hour. It nosedives somewhere about Santa Monica Beach, nice and handy for the Los Angeles based film makers. Lieutenant Hazen of the Federal Communications Commission and Lieutenant Bowers of the LA Police Department Homicide Squad join forces to find it. They lose sight of the space-suited alien invader when he strips off his protective garments – underneath he is invisible! Tests on the super-suit at the Griffith Park Planetarium prove that the creature is a life form based on silicon, rather than carbon, as you and I. Chased up a ladder and illuminated by infra-red beams, the Phantom materialises as a bald and bumpy fellow. He falls to his death and disintegrates, leaving nothing to show for it all.

COMMANDO CODY
SKY MARSHALL OF THE UNIVERSE
A REPUBLIC PICTURE
COUNTRY OF ORIGIN U. S. A.
53-1801

# Commando Cody: Sky Marshal of the Universe

*1953* Republic Pictures
*Producer* Herbert J. Yates
*Associate Producer* Franklin Adreon
*Directors* Fred C. Brannon, Harry Keller
*Story* Ronald Davidson
*Screenplay* Ronald Davidson, Barry Shipman
*Camera* Bud Thackery
*Special Effects* Howard and Theodore Lydecker
*Editors* Cliff Bell, Harold Minter
*Art Director* Frank Arrigo
12 episodes

Judd Holdren *Commando Cody*
Aline Towne *Joan Albright*
Gregory Gay *Retik the Ruler*
William Schallert *Ted Richards*
Lyle Talbot

*Episodes*

1. *Enemies of the Universe*
2. *Atomic Peril*
3. *Cosmic Vengeance*
4. *Nightmare Typhoon*
5. *War of the Space Giants*
6. *Destroyers of the Sun*
7. *Robot Monster from Mars*
8. *Hydrogen Hurricane*
9. *Solar Sky Riders*
10. *S.O.S. Ice Age*
11. *Lost in Outer Space*
12. *Captives of the Zero Hour*

Republic Pictures, home of Gene Autry, Roy Rogers and most of the other B-movie cowboys, was also the studio for serials throughout the Thirties and Forties. And most of these serials had science-fiction touches: as far back as 1936, yodelling cowpoke Autry found himself mixed up with the underground kingdom of *The Phantom Empire*. For this, their final serial, made with an eye to television, Republic hacked up all the best bits of three previous entries, *King of the Rocket Men* (1949), *Radar Men from the Moon* (1952) and *Zombies of the Stratosphere* (1952). All of these had featured a hero in a jet-propelled flying suit, and so, therefore, did Commando Cody. Same suit – different actor. This time it was Judd Holdren who slipped into the outfit previously buckled on by Tristram Coffin and George Wallace. After twelve twenty-minute half-hours, Commando finally put paid to Retik the Ruler of Mercury, played by a sinister chap called Gregory Gay. And after all that, the lobby card designer misspelled Cody's rank!

HALF MAN! HALF MONSTER!
HIMALAYAN MONSTER CAPTURED 20,000 FEET ABOVE THE EARTH!
Brought back alive . . . only to escape and leave a trail of death and destruction in the frightened city.
10,000 times stranger than the wildest fiction!
Millions gasped when they read about it in LIFE, TIME and ARGOSY Magazines!
One moment of romance in the midst of terror!
Dead men tell no tales!
Monster breaks loose, terrorizes city!
"SNOW CREATURE"
starring Paul LANGTON · Leslie DENISON · Teru SHIMADA · Rollin MORIYAMA · Produced by Directed by W. LEE WILDER
Story and Screenplay by MYLES WILDER · Released thru UNITED ARTISTS

# Snow Creature

*1954* Planet Filmways
*Distributor* United Artists
*Producer* W. Lee Wilder
*Director* W. Lee Wilder
*Screenplay* Myles Wilder
*Camera* Floyd Crosby
*Special Effects* Lee Zavitz
*Art Director* Frank Sylos
*Editor* Jodie Copelan
*Music* Manuel Compinsky
71 minutes

Paul Langton *Frank Parrish*
Leslie Denison *Peter Wells*
Teru Shimada *Subra*
Rollin Moriyama *Leva*
Robert Kino *Inspector Karma*
Darlene Fields *Joyce Parrish*
George Douglas *Coret Jr*
Robert Bice *Fleet*
Rudolph Anders *Dr Dupont*
Bill Phipps *Lt Dunbar*
Jack Daly *Edwards*
Robert Hinton *Manager*
Rusty Westcoatt *Guard*
Dick Sands *Creature*

'Ten Thousand Times Stranger than the Wildest Fiction!' screamed the lobby cards. 'Himalayan Monster Captured Twenty Thousand Feet Above the Earth!' Yes, friends, it was the Yeti, more popularly known as the Abominable Snowman. Behind the scenes were those Abominable Film-men, the Wilders. Not the famous satirist Billy, but his B-movie relatives, W. Lee and Myles, the fellows who brought you *Killers from Space* and *Phantom from Space*. Even the famous Phantom is here again. Dick Sands, the tall chap in the bald head and the Phantom costume, swaps spacesuit for furs and stalks the screen as the fabled Half Man-Half Monster. Paul Langton leads an expedition up the Himalayas, but when the wife of his sherpa guide is borne off by a Yeti, he refuses to pursue. The sherpa takes over and they catch a different Yeti, which is then crated up and posted to Los Angeles. Here the US Immigration Department won't let it in, so it busts out of its box and goes on the usual murderous rampage down the storm sewers. It gets shot, of course.

RAW PANIC
THE SCREEN HAS NEVER DARED REVEAL!
ALLIED ARTISTS presents
TARGET EARTH
Starring
RICHARD DENNING • KATHLEEN CROWLEY
VIRGINIA GREY • RICHARD REEVES featuring ROBERT ROARK
Produced by HERMAN COHEN • Directed by SHERMAN A. ROSE
Screenplay by BILL RAYNOR • An ABTCON PICTURES, Inc. Production

# Target Earth

'Raw Panic the Screen has Never Dared Reveal!' shrieked the lobby card – until the release of this sci-fi B-picture, apparently. Richard Denning, the man born to play Flash Gordon but who never did, and Kathleen Crowley make a good-looking pair of survivors in a Chicago which has been suddenly emptied of citizens. The cause of the evacuation is an invasion by clawed robots from the planet Venus equipped with death-rays in their hands. In the original magazine story, *Deadly City,* these aliens are fragile, shadowy wraiths who drop dead as soon as they breathe Earth's atmosphere. Thus does Hollywood improve on originals. Screenwriter Bill Raynor improved their ultimate destruction, too. It takes all the scientific knowhow of Dr Whit Bissell to thwart the stompers with supersonic soundwaves that crack their glass faceplates. There's a different ending, too. Instead of the holed-up heroes returning to their normal lives, everybody dies except Richard Denning and Kathleen Crowley, our brand new Adam and Eve!

*1954* Abtcon Pictures
*Distributor* Allied Artists
*Producer* Herman Cohen
*Director* Sherman A. Rose
*Story* based on the novel *Deadly City* by Ivar Jorgenson
*Screenplay* Bill Raynor
*Camera* Guy Roe
*Special Effects* David Koehler
*Art Director* James Sullivan
*Editor* Sherman A. Rose
*Music* Paul Dunlap
75 minutes

Richard Denning *Frank Brooks*
Kathleen Crowley *Nora King*
Virginia Grey *Vicki Harris*
Richard Reeves *Jim Wilson*
Robert Roark *Davis*
Mort Marshall *Otis*
Arthur Space *General*
White Bissell *Scientist*
Jim Drake *Lieutenant*
Steve Pendleton *Colonel*
House Peters Jr *Technician*

CONQUEST OF SPACE
COLOR BY TECHNICOLOR
PRODUCED BY GEORGE PAL
DIRECTED BY BYRON HASKIN
SCREENPLAY BY JAMES O'HANLON
ADAPTATION BY PHILIP YORDAN,
BARRE LYNDON AND
GEORGE WORTHINGTON YATES
BASED ON THE BOOK BY
CHESLEY BONESTELL AND WILLY LEY
A PARAMOUNT PICTURE

# Conquest of Space

*1955* Paramount Pictures
*Producer* George Pal
*Director* Byron Haskin
*Story* from the book by
Chesley Bonestell, Willy Ley
*Screenplay* James O'Hanlon
*Adaptation* Philip Yordan, Barré Lyndon,
George Worthing Yates
*Camera* Lionel Lindon
*Special Effects* John P. Fulton,
Irmin Roberts,
Paul Lerpae, Ivyl Burks,
Jan Domela
*Art Directors* Hal Periera,
Joseph MacMillan Johnson
*Music* Van Cleave
*Editor* Everett Douglas
*Astronomical Art* Chesley Bonestell
*Technical Advisor* Werner von Braun
81 minutes Technicolor

Walter Brooke *Col Samuel Merritt*
Eric Fleming *Capt Barney Merritt*
Mickey Shaughnessey *Sgt Mahoney*
Phil Foster *Jackie Siegle*
Benson Fong *Sgt Imoto*
Russ Martin *Andre Fodor*
William Redfield *Roy Cooper*
William Hopper *Dr George Fenton*
Vito Scotti *Sanella*
John Dennis *Donkersgoed*
Michael Fox *Elsbach*
Joan Shawlee *Rosie*
Iphigenie Castiglioni *Mrs Fodor*
Rosemary Clooney *Herself*

George (Georg) Pal, the pioneering papa of modern movie sci-fi (he showed the way in 1950 with his *Destination Moon)*, had a final fling at highly technicolored semi-documentaries by bringing to life Chesley Bonestell's famed astronomical illustrations in *Conquest of Space*. Pal was also the pioneer of Puppetoons, also made for Paramount, and unfortunately it shows once again, as plastic acting by unknowns fails to touch the interest of the audience. 'There are some things that man is not meant to do', intones the Colonel in charge of this space project, thus expressing an unlikely attitude for a commanding officer coupled with good advice for those considering paying to see this film. Actually, the Special Effects are worth the money: meteorite hits circling space station; space ship rockets off to red-dusted Mars and back.

CREATURE
WITH THE ATOM BRAIN
Starring RICHARD DENNING with ANGELA STEVENS
Story and Screen Play by CURT SIODMAK • Directed by EDWARD L. CAHN • A CLOVER PRODUCTION
A COLUMBIA PICTURE

# Creature with the Atom Brain

*1955* Clover Productions
*Distributor* Columbia Pictures
*Producer* Sam Katzman
*Director* Edward L. Cahn
*Screenplay* Curt Siodmak
*Camera* Fred Jackman Jr
*Editor* Aaron Stell
*Music* Mischa Bakeleinikoff
*Art Director* Paul Palmentola
*Special Effects* Jack Erickson
69 minutes

Richard Denning *Dr Chet Walker*
Angela Stevens *Joyce Walker*
John Launer *Capt Dave Harris*
Michael Granger *Frank Buchanan*
Gregory Gay *Prof Steigg*
Linda Bennet *Penny Walker*
Tristram Coffin *D.A. MacGraw*
Harry Lauter *Reporter*
Charles Evans *Chief Camden*
Pierre Watkin *Mayor Bremer*
Lane Chandler *General Saunders*
Nelson Leigh *Dr Kenneth Notron*
Don Harvey *Lester Banning*
Paul Hoffman *Dunn*
Edward Coch *Jason Franchot*
Karl Davis *Creature*
Charles Horvath *Creature*

Sam Katzman and Curt Siodmak make a curious combination, and a curious movie. The former was king of the B's and the serials in an earlier era, while the latter is a respected science-fiction screenwriter who ran the gamut from Germany in the Thirties *(F.P. One)* to the States *(Donovan's Brain* and *The Wolf Man).* Joining forces for the money, they gave this old-fashioned zombie story a sci-fi twist. Siodmak brought his sophistication and Katzman brought his stalwart team of serial actors, plus a few reels of handy action. Frank Buchanan, deported mobster, returns secretly and finances the crazed Professor Steigg in his plan to produce atomically controlled zombies. Dr Chet Walker, handsome head of the Police Laboratory, investigates, but his partner, Captain Dave Harris, gets the treatment via a headful of electrodes. Trains crash, factories explode, until Katzman finally runs out of stock footage and the zombies are destroyed.

TERRIFYING! FANTASTIC! STARTLING!
KING DINOSAUR
MIGHTIEST MONSTER OF THEM ALL!
SEE... A PREHISTORIC WORLD OF FANTASTIC ADVENTURE COME TO LIFE!
Starring
BILL BRYANT · WANDA CURTIS
with
DOUGLAS HENDERSON · PATTI GALLAGHER
Produced by AL ZIMBALIST and BERT I. GORDON
Directed by BERT I. GORDON
Screenplay by TOM GRIES

# *King Dinosaur*

*1955* Zimgor Productions
*Distributor* Lippert Pictures
*Producers* Al Zimbalist and Bert I. Gordon
*Director* Bert I. Gordon
*Story* Bert I. Gordon, Al Zimbalist
*Screenplay* Tom Gries
*Photography* Gordon Avil
*Special Effects* Bert I. Gordon
*Editors* Jack Cornwall, John Bushelman
*Music* Mischa Terr
63 minutes

Bill Bryant *Dr Ralph Martin*
Wanda Curtis *Dr Patricia Bennett*
Douglas Hendersen *Richard Gordon*
Patti Gallagher *Nora Pierce*
Marvin Miller *Narrator*

This hour-long B-minus movie was made (produced, directed, written and special-effected) by Bert I. Gordon, the man who used his initials to brand himself as Hollywood's 'Mister BIG'. Gordon made quite a few sci-fi B's, all of them using the same methods – parading his actors in front of process screens – and most of them using the same stock footage on those process screens – the prehistoric monsters sequence from Hal Roach's popular 1939 epic, *One Million BC*. This flick was no different from the rest, except that the dinosaur footage takes place on another planet, a spot which strongly resembles the foothills around Los Angeles. As the synopsis states, 'When a new star named Nova settles in the Earth's galaxy, a half-year's rocket flight away, feverish plans are made to send an expedition of four to the new planet'. (Well, is it a star or a planet?) A pair of doctors, one handsome, the other pretty, set off for six months in their superimposed V-2 rocket, and land by a lake. Here their camp is raided by a small honeybear they christen Little Joe. Finally the scientists set off an atomic explosion to rid themselves of Gordon's back-projection screen. The most original thing in the film is the name of the production company: Zimgor – half a Zimbalist and half a Gordon, see?

Destroying...
Terrifying!
5
THE BEAST WITH 1,000,000 EYES!
WIDE SCREEN
TERROR-SCOPE
with
PAUL BIRCH · LORNA THAYER · DONA COLE · and the BEAST
Produced & Directed by DAVID KRAMARSKY · Screenplay by TOM FILER · A SAN MATEO PICTURE · Presented by PALO ALTO PRODUCTIONS
RELEASED BY
American
RELEASING CORPORATION

# The Beast with 1,000,000 Eyes

*1955* San Mateo Pictures/
Palo Alto Productions
*Distributor* American Releasing Corp
*Producer* David Kramarsky
*Director* David Kramarsky
*Screenplay* Tom Filer
*Camera* Everett Baker
*Special Effects* Paul Blaisdell
*Editor* Jack Killeser
*Music* John Bickford
78 minutes

Paul Birch *Allan Kelly*
Lorna Thayer *Carol Kelly*
Dona Cole *Sandy Kelly*
Paul Blaisdell *The Beast*
Dick Sargent *Larry*
Leonard Traver *Him*
Chester Conklin *Old Man Webber*

'Destroying! Terrifying' came this bottom-rung B-movie, filmed, it says here, in 'Wide Screen Terror-Scope'! Monochrome, of course. Paul Birch, promoted from lower-rung character roles to temporary stardom, played Dad of a small family (just the three of them) living the lonely life in a desert. Perhaps that's why Mr and Mrs Kelly call their small daughter Sandy. Nearby is an aged refugee from Mack Sennett's Keystone Kops of 1911, Chester Conklin, whose last big role was caught in the cogs of Charlie Chaplin's *Modern Times* (1936). Down comes an alien invader from up there, with a plan to conquer the Earth. This it does by beginning small – it takes over the minds of birds – and working its way up to dogs. Then it has a go at taking control of the local idiot, a no-name farmhand they all call 'Him'. Finally, as it gets round to cows, the Kelly family thwart it with a concentrated dose of the power of love. This kills the creature – or does it? What about that bunny-rabbit hopping sinisterly behind the end titles?

The explanation of the catch-penny title is that the Million Eyes belonged to the animals taken over by the mind of the Beast!

M·G·M
PRESENTS
FORBIDDEN PLANET
IN CINEMASCOPE AND COLOR
STARRING
WALTER PIDGEON · ANNE FRANCIS · LESLIE NIELSEN
With
WARREN STEVENS
And Introducing
ROBBY, THE ROBOT
Screen Play by CYRIL HUME · Based on a Story by IRVING BLOCK and ALLEN ADLER · Photographed in EASTMAN COLOR
Directed by FRED McLEOD WILCOX
Produced by NICHOLAS NAYFACK
AN M-G-M PICTURE
AMAZING!

# Forbidden Planet

*1956* Metro-Goldwyn-Mayer
*Producer* Nicholas Nayfack
*Director* Fred McLeod Wilcox
*Story* Irving Block, Allen Adler
*Screenplay* Cyril Hume
*Camera* George Folsey
*Special Effects* Arnold Gillespie, Glen Robinson, A.D. Flowers, Dean Pearson, Logan Frazee, Joe Zomar, Irving Reis, Jack McMasters
*Art Directors* Arthur Lonergan, Mentor Huebner, Arnold Gillespie, Irving Block
*Animation Effects* Josh Meador, Dwight Carlisle, Joe Alves
*Monster Design* Ken Hultgren
*Electronic Music* Louis and Bebe Barron
106 minutes Eastmancolor Cinemascope

Walter Pidgeon *Dr Edward Morbius*
Anne Francis *Altaira Morbius*
Leslie Nielsen *Cdr John Adams*
Warren Stevens *Lt Doc Ostrow*
Jack Kelly *Lt Jerry Farman*
Richard Anderson *Chief Quinn*
Earl Holliman *Cookie*
George Wallace *Bosun*
Jimmy Thomson *Youngerford*
James Drury *Joe Strong*
Harry Harvey Jr *Randall*
Roger McGee *Lindstrom*
Peter Miller *Moran*
Morgan Jones *Nichols*
Richard Grant *Silvers*
Les Tremayne *Narrator*
Frankie Carpenter/
Frankie Darro *Robby the Robot*

One word was thought enough to describe MGM's major assault on science-fiction: 'Amazing!' Robby the Robot may appear to be carrying off leggy Anne Francis for some sort of mechanical purpose for which he has not been provided with the necessary tool, but that is just bring-em-in lobby card art. The film is, of all things, a clever variation on *The Tempest* by William Shakespeare. Unhinged super-scientist Morbius (Walter Pidgeon) replaces Prospero the wizard, his fair-haired daughter Altaira (Miss Francis) pinch-hits for Miranda, the maid who has never known a man, and Robby the Robot subs for the creature Caliban. We are in the 23rd Century. Commander John J. Adams and his crew of the United Planets Cruiser C-57-D are seeking the whereabouts of the prospecting mission ship *Bellerophon*, lost on the fourth planet of the red star Altair. So much for setting-up. Once landed and made at home by the inhospitable Morbius, former philologist of the previous expedition, planetary wonders unfold before their eyes, ranging from the self-perpetuating civilisation of the long-gone Krel, to the venerable scientist's beautiful but very virginal daughter, Altaira. Leslie Neilson, dead-pan as ever but then humourless, has an heroic confrontation with Walter Pidgeon's Id, an invisible monster animated by the lads from Walt Disney's Studio, while Robby the Robot went on to star in a film called *The Invisible Boy* (1957).

WORLD
Without
END
CINEMASCOPE
TECHNICOLOR
starring
HUGH MARLOWE
NANCY GATES
AN ALLIED ARTISTS PICTURE
PRODUCED BY
RICHARD HEERMANCE
WRITTEN AND DIRECTED BY
EDWARD BERNDS

# World Without End

*1956* Allied Artists
*Producer* Richard Heermance
*Director* Edward Bernds
*Screenplay* Edward Bernds
*Camera* Ellsworth Fredericks
*Editor* Eda Warren
*Art Director* David Milton
*Music* Leith Stevens
79 minutes Technicolor CinemaScope

Hugh Marlowe *Borden*
Nacy Gates *Garnet*
Nelson Leigh *Galbraithe*
Rod Taylor *Ellis*
Shawn Smith *Elaine*
Lisa Montell *Deens*
Christopher Dark *Jaffe*
Booth Colman *Mories*
Everett Glass *Timmek*
Stanley Fraser *Elda*
William Vedder *James*
Rankin Mansfield *Beryl*
Paul Brinegar *Vida*
Mickey Simpson *Naga*

The year is 1957, nine months ahead of the release date of this movie. Four astronauts on a test flight to Mars orbit the planet and return home to Earth. By accident they break through the Time Barrier and land home in the year 2508! Naturally, according to the feelings of the Fifties, Earth has been decimated by atomic warfare. On the surface live Mutants, one-eyed survivors of the nuclear holocaust. Underground exists the dying race of fairly normal folk, especially the girls, who take a fancy to the virile spacemen. Despite all Booth Colman, the leading brain, can do, the men from yesterday help the undergrounders in the war against the Mutants, demolishing a giant spider to boot. Unable to return to their past, the astronauts elect to help the girls build a better tomorrow. Not bad, considering it was written and directed by an ex-Three Stooges man.

NOW! THE TRUTH ABOUT FLYING SAUCERS!
You'll see his "top secret" films of them for the first time!
This radar screen "captured" them over Washington, D.C.
He "caught" them with his camera!
This plane crashed trying to catch them!
He almost collided with one of them!
This jet fought a fantastic dogfight with one of them!
SEE IT ALL AS IT ACTUALLY HAPPENED!...and is still happening!
THE MOTION PICTURE SCOOP OF THE CENTURY!
UFO
CLARENCE GREENE and RUSSELL ROUSE present
UNIDENTIFIED FLYING OBJECTS
Written by FRANCIS MARTIN · Produced by CLARENCE GREENE · Directed by WINSTON JONES · Released thru United Artists
With the people who actually lived the story of the U. F. O.

# Unidentified Flying Objects

*1956* Greene-Rouse Productions
*Distributor* United Artists
*Producer* Clarence Greene
*Co-Producer* Russell Rouse
*Associate Producer* Fernando Carrere
*Director* Winston Jones
*Screenplay* Francis Martin
*Camera* Howard Anderson
*Editor* Chester Schaeffer
*Music* Ernest Gold
*Music Director* Emil Newman
92 minutes b/w with colour sequences

Tom Powers *Albert M. Chop*

Possibly the greatest tribute this film received was that it was not included in the *Aurum Encyclopedia of Science Fiction Films*. Somebody up there takes it seriously. Which, of course, is exactly what the respected film-making team of Clarence Greene and Russell Rouse intended. It was a somewhat overlong documentary running an hour and a half, the first forty minutes of which failed to show a single saucer. Tom Powers, veteran from the long lost silent movie days, portrayed real-life Albert M. Chop, the ex-newspaper man who became the head of the Press Section of Air Material Command. He was personally involved in Project Bluebook, the USAAF's official designation for the secret investigation of UFOs, as Unidentified Flying Objects came quickly to be called. Actual footage filmed of some of the odd objects is eventuallly shown, but the quality, being substandard 16-millimetre in the main, of both images and colour, makes the big-screen blow-ups disappointing. Seen were sightings made in Montana in 1950, Utah in 1952, and Washington DC. Shaky stuff, but enough to convince some, including the film-makers, that there might indeed be more to the current UFO craze that meets the earthly eye. As the film asked: 'Who are they? Where are they from? Who made them?' We still don't know.

FROM A LOST AGE... TERROR CRAWLS FROM THE DEPTHS OF THE EARTH!
The MOLE PEOPLE
STARRING JOHN AGAR · CYNTHIA PATRICK
with HUGH BEAUMONT · NESTOR PAIVA · ALAN NAPIER
Directed by VIRGIL VOGEL · Written by LASZLO GOROG · Produced by WILLIAM ALLAND · A UNIVERSAL-INTERNATIONAL PICTURE

# The Mole People

*1956* Universal-International
*Producer* William Alland
*Director* Virgil Vogel
*Screenplay* Laszlo Gorog
*Camera* Ellis Carter
*Special Effects* Clifford Stine
*Art Director* Alexander Golitzen
*Editor* Irving Birnbaum
*Music* Hans J. Salter
*Makeup* Bud Westmore, Jack Kevan
77 minutes

John Agar *Dr Roger Bentley*
Cynthia Patrick *Adad*
Hugh Beaumont *Dr Jud Bellamin*
Nestor Paiva *Etienne Lafarge*
Alan Napier *Elinu*
Robin Hughes *First Officer*
Phil Chambers *Dr Paul Stuart*
Arthur Gilmour *Sharu*
Rodd Redwing *Nazar*
Yvonne de Lavallade *Dancer*
James Logan *Officer*
John Dodsworth *Priest*
Joseph Abdullah *Arab*
Dr Frank Baxter *Narrator*

Jolly old John Agar is Dr Roger Bentley, head of an anthropological expedition in Asia, where the discovery of an odd ancient artifact takes them to a mountain top in search of a lost tribe of Sumerians. One of the party promptly falls down a hole, and John and Co spend some time clambering down to save him. An earth tremor seals them in, and further exploration brings them face to pasty face with the Sumarians. These albinos live in unpleasant partnership with the Mole Men, curious burrowing creatures who have to be frequently whipped. Elinu, the ruler of the small supply of Sumerians (only 150 of them remain), puts on a dance for the outsiders as a prelude to a ritual sacrifice of virgins to the Eye of Ishtar. This is a shaft of sunlight from outside, which has the effect of charring the virgins to death. However, it does prove to be a way out for Agar and Co, who have tired of eating nothing but mushrooms. Advertised as 'Horror Crawls from the Depths of the Earth', for reasons unknown the lobby card was censored, so that it now reads, thanks to sticky-paper – 'Terror'.

The Land Unknown
CinemaScope
STARRING
WILLIAM REYNOLDS
SHAWN SMITH
JOCK MAHONEY
with HENRY BRANDON
PHIL HARVEY
DOUGLAS KENNEDY
Directed by VIRGIL VOGEL
Screenplay by LASZLO GOROG
Produced by WILLIAM ALLAND
Universal International
A UNIVERSAL-INTERNATIONAL PICTURE

# The Land Unknown

*1957* Universal International
*Producer* William Alland
*Director* Virgil Vogel
*Story* Charles Palmer
*Screenplay* Laszlo Gorog
*Adaptation* William Robson
*Camera* Ellis W. Carter
*Special Effects* Clifford Stine, Fred Knoth, Jack Kevan, Roswell Hoffman
*Art Director* Richard Riedel, Alexander Golitzen
*Editor* Fred McDowell
*Music* Joseph Gershenson
78 minutes Cinemascope

William Reynolds *Lt Jack Carmen*
Shawn Smith *Maggie Hathaway*
Jock Mahoney *Cdr Hal Roberts*
Henry Brandon *Dr Charles Hunter*
Phil Harvey *Steve Miller*
Douglas Kennedy *Capt Burnham*

You can blame this film on Admiral Byrd. Back in 1947 he found a warm water area in icebound Antarctica. Or you can blame MGM, who made a documentary about it called *The Land That Time Forgot*. It's clips from that film you can see in this film, with a model helicopter superimposed. In this special effect fly Commander Jock Mahoney, tall enough for Tarzan, which he was; William Reynolds and Phil Harvey, stalwarts all of the United States Navy, plus Shawn Smith, obligatory pretty girl reporter. The year is now 1957 and they are off down very south for an anniversary exploration. Starting well – their helicopter collides with a prehistoric pterodactyl – they crashland into the Mesozoic Era and encounter not only a Tyranosaurus Rex, but a long-necked Elasmosaurus, too. Exploring ever deeper they encounter the most fearsome monster of them all, a mad scientist left over from the Byrd Expedition. To make matters worse, he is played by Henry Brandon, the crooked man 'Barnaby' from Laurel and Hardy's fairy-tail exploit, *Babes in Toyland*. Brandon keeps the dinosaurs at bay by blowing his horn and smashing their eggs. Using bits of Brandon's abandoned aircraft, Mahoney & Co rebuild their 'copter and fly away home.

SUPER-
QUAKE
TILTS
THE
EARTH!
THE
NIGHT
THE WORLD
EXPLODED!
starring KATHRYN GRANT · WILLIAM LESLIE
Written by JACK NATTEFORD and LUCI WARD · Produced by SAM KATZMAN
Directed by FRED F. SEARS · A CLOVER PRODUCTION · A COLUMBIA PICTURE

# The Night the World Exploded

*1957* Clover Productions
*Distributor* Columbia Pictures
*Producer* Sam Katzman
*Director* Fred F. Sears
*Screenplay* Jack Natteford, Luci Ward
*Camera* Benjamin H. Kline
*Art Director* Paul Palmentola
*Editor* Paul Borofsky
*Music* Ross DiMaggio
64 minutes

Kathryn Grant *Laura Hutchinson*
William Leslie *Dr David Conway*
Tristram Coffin *Dr Ellis Morton*
Raymond Greenleaf *Governor Cheyney*
Charles Evans *General Bates*
Frank Scannell *Sheriff Quinn*
Marshall Reed *Aide*
Fred Coby *Ranger Brown*
Paul Savage *Ranger Kirk*
Terry Frost *Foreman*

Tristram Coffin, stalwart of many a semi sci-fi serial, is the clue to the origins of this hour-long sci-fi saga, produced by Sam Katzman, legendary guardian of the tight purse. Seismologist William Leslie, second-billed to his attractive assistant, Kathryn Grant, invents a Pressure Photometer, a gadget for predicting earthquakes. As the incidence of these eruptions is on the increase, the scientists shift their equipment to the Carlsbad Caverns, that well-loved location for sci-fi films deep in the heart of New Mexico. Sure enough, there it is: black stones which rise up from the centre of the Earth like cream in a bottle of milk. As long as the stones stay under water, all is okay, but once exposed to nitrogen they expand, heat up and explode. Leslie christens this unknown element E-112, and why not? As the stones are bobbing up all over the world, floods are instigated by means of stock footage. This helps, but one final, major volcano is forming in Nevada. The only answer is to use the E-112 to blast a dam, divert a river, flood the volcano, and save the planet. So that's what they do.

HOWCO INTERNATIONAL presents
THE BRAIN from PLANET AROUS
STARRING
JOHN AGAR · JOYCE MEADOWS · ROBERT FULLER
WITH THOMAS B. HENRY · KENNETH TERRELL · HENRY TRAVIS
PRODUCED BY JACQUES MARQUETTE · DIRECTED BY NATHAN HERTZ
A MARQUETTE PRODUCTION · RELEASED BY HOWCO INTERNATIONAL

# The Brain from Planet Arous

*1957* Marquette Productions
*Distributor* Howco International
*Producer* Jacques Marquette
*Director* Nathan Hertz
*Screenplay* Ray Buffam
*Camera* Jacques Marquette
*Editor* Irving Schoenberg
*Music* Walter Greene
70 minutes

John Agar *Steve*
Joyce Meadows *Sally Fallon*
Robert Fuller *Dan*
Thomas Brown Henry *John Fallon*
Kenneth Terrell *Colonel*
Henry Travis *Col. Frogley*
Tom Graham *Sheriff Paine*
Leslie Thomas *General Brown*
Bill Giorgio *Russian*

Hunky John Agar again, this time as the handsome but isolated (for reasons of budget) scientist who one day wakes up to find his head is occupied by a flying brain from outer space. It blows in, semi-transparently, from that well-known planet Arous and, what's more, its name is Gor! Agar's pleasant girlfriend, Joyce Meadows, suspects something is wrong with her loved one when he goes a bit glassy-eyed and starts bringing down airplanes at a glance. Fortunately for all, a second semi-transparent brain wafts into their shack. This time it is a nice brain, name of Vol. Vol tells Joyce the secret of how to deal with the situation. Give John a sharp boff on the noggin! What else remains to be said, except – Gor!

LIFE MAGAZINE SAYS — "THE ULTIMATE IN SCIENTIFIC MONSTERS"
REACTOR BALANCE
WAR of the SATELLITES
starring
DICK MILLER · SUSAN CABOT · RICHARD DEVON · Produced & Directed by ROGER CORMAN · Screenplay by LAWRENCE LOUIS GOLDMAN
Co-producers JACK RABIN and IRVING BLOCK · From a Story by IRVING BLOCK and JACK RABIN · AN ALLIED ARTISTS PICTURE

# War of the Satellites

*1958* Allied Artists
*Producer* Roger Corman
*Co-Producers* Jack Rabin, Irving Block
*Director* Roger Corman
*Story* Jack Rabin, Irving Block
*Screenplay* Lawrence Louis Goldman
*Camera* Floyd Crosby
*Special Effects* Jack Rabin, Irving Block, Louis DeWitt
*Art Director* Daniel Haller
*Editor* Irene Morra
*Music* Walter Greene
64 minutes

Dick Miller *Dave Boyer*
Susan Cabot *Sybil Carrington*
Richard Devon *Dr Van Pander*
Eric Sinclair *Dr Lazar*
Michael Fox *Akad*
Robert Shayne *Hodgkins*
Jerry Barclay *John*
Jay Saver *Jay*
Mitzi McCall *Mitzi*
John Brinkley *Crew*

Roger Corman, bright young man of the B-flicks, inspired by Russia's first Sputnik in space, whipped this little number up in a week and a day and had it rushing round the cinemas within two months. Unfortunately the film looks like it, with the special effects sequences shot separately from the actors to save time, and seldom combining. It should have been better, as the chaps who contrived the effects also wrote the story and co-produced. Folks at the United Nations Satellite programme decide to send a manned rocket into space. Unfortunately, minds other than theirs think otherwise, and set up an impenetrable barrier, warning the UN that should they continue their schemes, Earth itself will be destroyed. Doctor Van Pander, the scientist in charge of the experiment, gets killed in a car crash, and the brains from beyond revive his corpse, controlling him as the instrument of their powers. This super-zombie is almost successful in causing a second UN rocket to crash into the barrier, but fortunately he is overcome at the vital moment by one of the crew, Dave Boyer. This leaves the way clear for space exploration, apparently, plus fulfilment for Boyer with the mathematician he loves.

ROCKET INTO NEW ORBITS OF THRILLS WITH
SPACE MASTER X-7
...piercing new worlds of TERROR!
starring
BILL WILLIAMS · LYN THOMAS · ROBERT ELLIS
A REGALSCOPE PICTURE
PRODUCED BY BERNARD GLASSER · DIRECTED BY EDWARD BERNDS · WRITTEN BY GEORGE WORTHING YATES and DANIEL MAINWARING
A REGAL FILMS, Inc. PRODUCTION · Released by 20th CENTURY-FOX

## Space Master X-7

*1958* Regal Films
*Distributor* Twentieth Century Fox
*Producer* Bernard Glasser
*Director* Edward Bernds
*Screenplay* George Worthing Yates, Daniel Mainwaring
*Camera* Brydon Baker
*Editor* John Link
*Music* Josef Zimanich
71 minutes Regalscope

Bill Williams *John Hand*
Lyn Thomas *Lora Greeling*
Robert Ellis *Radigan*
Paul Frees *Charles Palmer*
Joan Barry *Miss Stevens*
Thomas Browne Henry *Prof West*
Fred Sherman *Morse*
Jesse Kirkpatrick *Captain*
Moe Howard *Cab Driver*
Rhoda Williams *Miss Archer*
Carole Varga *Elaine Frohman*
Thomas Wilde *Collins*
Greg Martell *Engineer*
Court Shepherd *Chief Hendry*

'Piercing New Worlds of Terror!' was the curious phrase featured on the lobby cards for this film, the lower half of a double bill topped by *The Fly*. Buckle-browed boy-next-door Bill Williams and his buddy, Robert Ellis, play United States Security Agents who are alerted to locate a space probe that returns to Earth after a trip to Mars, covered alien fungus. Scientist Paul Frees discovers the stuff and locks it in his laboratory. Naming it the Blood Rust – when mixed with rust the fungus grows rapidly and enormously, devouring anything and everything in its path – Frees falls victim to it. Then the stuff takes over the body of Frees' former fiancee, Lyn Thomas, and the nationwide hunt is on. Fortunately Bill mixes a decontaminating antidote which clears up the fungus and restores Miss Thomas to her normal pleasant self. The most startling thing about the film, however, was the guest star appearance of Moe Howard, the one of the Three Stooges with the fringe on top, as a taxi driver. This may have had something to do with the fact that the director, Edward Bernds, had cut his comedic teeth on Stooges shorts.

MANKIND'S
FIRST
FLIGHT TO
VENUS
-- the Female
Planet!
QUEEN OF
OUTER SPACE
COLOR BY DELUXE CINEMASCOPE
STARRING
ZSA ZSA GABOR
WITH
ERIC FLEMING · LAURIE MITCHELL · LISA DAVIS
From a Story by BEN HECHT • Produced by BEN SCHWALB • Directed by EDWARD BERNDS • Screenplay by CHARLES BEAUMONT
AN ALLIED ARTISTS Picture

# Queen of Outer Space

*1958* Allied Artists
*Producer* Ben Schwalb
*Director* Edward Bernds
*Story* Ben Hecht
*Screenplay* Charles Beaumont
*Camera* William Whitley
*Art Editor* David Milton
*Editor* William Austin
*Music* Marlin Skiles
*Wardrobe* Irene Caine
*Makeup* Emile Lavigne
80 minutes Deluxe Color Cinemascope

ZsaZsa Gabor *Talleah*
Eric Fleming *Capt Neil Patterson*
Laurie Mitchell *Queen Yllana*
Lisa Davis *Motiya*
Paul Birch *Prof Konrad*
Barbara Darrow *Kaeel*
Dave Willo *Lt Michael Cruze*
Patrick Waltz *Lt Harry Turner*
Marilyn Buford *Odeena*
Marjorie Durant *Amazon*
Lynn Cartwright *Guard*
Mary Ford *Guard*
Tania Velia *Councillor*

1985 was 27 years in the future when this send-up of the sci-fi craze was produced. This was the year husky Eric Fleming and his All-American astronauts were rocketed up to a space station to check on the recent mysterious destruction of several space bases. As they leave the station, it is exploded, and the boys are buzzed up to the planet Venus. The lobby cards call it 'The Female Planet', and so it proves, for they are taken prisoner by Queen Yllana and her Amazons. The Queen wears a blank mask to cover her hideous disfigurement while she plans to destroy Earth with her Disintegrator Ray. Fortunately for the men, in several ways, ZsaZsa Gabor and her glamour girls are about, and save the day and the men. DeLuxe Color and CinemaScope come in handy to cope with the ladies of Venus, a line-up that would not look lost on the runway at the Windmill. The picture was crafted, if that is the word, by no lesser talents than those of Ben Hecht, once scriptwriter of many a Hollywood major, and Edward Bernds, a director more usually found in the company of the Three Stooges.

THE TOWERING
TERROR FROM
HELL!
Admitted.
SEE A SIXTY-FOOT GIANT DESTROYED ... IN COLOR!
TWA
WAR OF THE COLOSSAL BEAST
starring
SALLY FRASER · ROGER PACE · DEAN PARKIN · Produced and Directed by BERT I. GORDON
Screenplay by GEORGE WORTHINGTON YATES · From a Story by BERT I. GORDON
A JAMES H. NICHOLSON and SAMUEL Z. ARKOFF Production · An AMERICAN-INTERNATIONAL Picture

# War of the Colossal Beast

*UK title* The Terror Strikes
*1958* American International
*Executive Producers* James H. Nicholson, Samuel Z. Arkoff
*Producer* Bert I. Gordon
*Director* Bert I. Gordon
*Story* Bert I. Gordon
*Screenplay* George Worthing Yates
*Camera* Jack Marta
*Special Effects* Bert I. Gordon
*Editor* Ronald Sinclair
*Music* Albert Glasser
68 minutes color sequence

Sally Fraser *Joyce Manning*
Roger Pace *Major Baird*
Dean Parkin *Col Glenn Manning*
Russ Bender *Dr Carmichael*
Charles Stewart *Capt Harris*
George Becwar *Swanson*
Robert Hernandez *Miguel*
Rico Alaniz *Sgt Luis Murillo*
George Alexander *Officer*
George Navarro *Doctor*
John McNamara *Neurologist*
Bob Garnet *Correspondent*
Ray Gordon *Major*
George Milan *General Nelson*
Bill Giorgio *Bus Driver*
Loretta Nicholson *Joan*
June Jocelyn *Mother*
Stan Chambers *TV Announcer*
Jack Kosslyn *TV Newscaster*

In 1957 Bert I. Gordon, a name to reckon with among the B-picture people of Hollywood, wrote, produced and directed *The Amazing Colossal Man* – a title he thought of after seeing Universal's *The Incredible Shrinking Man*. 'Mr BIG's' reversal procedure made enough money for the obvious sequel, a sequel. Hence *The War of the Colossal Beast*. Unfortunately for Bert, his original star, Glenn Langan, had had quite enough of stomping near-naked (including hair loss from the head) and uprooting cardboard cut-outs of buildings. But our man was nonplussed. Indeed he was plussed, for by casting another tall actor, Dean Parkin, and blasting most of his face away with a shell, nobody but the brightest buff noticed. Even when he padded out the new picture with a reel or two of footage from the earlier affair. 'The Towering Terror from Hell' (*vide* lobby card) survives a fatal fall from Boulder Dam, whither he has been blown by Army gunfire following exposure to a plutonium bomb which has caused him to grow ten feet a day. (Er – ten feet *tall*, that is.) So much for the first film. This continuance of the yarn follows much the same pattern, save that the Towering Terror now has only half a face. This time he ends up, and finally we are happy to say, by walking into some high tension wires. 'See a Sixty-foot Giant Destroyed . . . in Color!' cried the lobby-cards, spoiling the surprise climax. The rest of the film was in black-and-white.

DOLL DWARFS versus
the CRUSHING GIANT BEASTS!
PAINT
PAINT
AX-5701
ATTACK OF THE PUPPET PEOPLE
starring JOHN AGAR · JOHN HOYT · JUNE KENNEY · Produced and Directed by BERT I. GORDON
Screenplay by GEORGE WORTHINGTON YATES · From a Story by BERT I. GORDON · A JAMES H. NICHOLSON and SAMUEL Z. ARKOFF Production · AN AMERICAN-INTERNATIONAL PICTURE

# Attack of the Puppet People

*1958* American International
*Executive Producers* James H. Nicholson, Samuel Z. Arkoff
*Producer* Bert I. Gordon
*Director* Bert I. Gordon
*Story* Bert I. Gordon
*Screenplay* George Worthing Yates
*Camera* Ernst Laszlo
*Special Effects* Bert I. Gordon
*Editor* Ronald Sinclair
*Music* Albert Glasser
78 minutes

John Agar *Bob Wesley*
John Hoyt *Mr Franz*
June Kenney *Sally Reynolds*
Michael Mark *Emil*
Jack Kosslyn *Sgt Patterson*
Marlene Willis *Laurie*
Ken Miller *Stan*
Laurie Mitchell *Georgia*
Scott Peters *Mac*
Susan Gordon *Agnes*
June Joceyln *Brownie Leader*
Jean Moorhead *Janet*
Hank Patterson *Doorman*
Hal Bogart *Mailman*
Troy Patterson *Elevator Man*
Bill Giorgio *Janitor*
George Diestel *Switchboard Man*
Jaime Forster *Ernie*
Mark Lowell *Salesman*

'Doll Dwarfs versus the Crushing Giant Beasts!' was the promise for this overlong B-movie bearing one star name to boost – John Agar, the former Mr Shirley Temple. Agar became quite a regular semi-star of low budget sci-fi films, mainly because they were all he was offered. Here he is one of six, three male, three female, who are shrunk by unbalanced puppeteer and doll-maker, John Hoyt, in his search for human but pocketable company. The 'Crushing Giant Beasts' are back-projected cats and the like, Bert I. Gordon's usual way of making his actors look small. Fortunately, George Worthing Yates, who specialised in science-fiction scripts, enlarged Gordon's original story.

FROM
TIME UNBORN...
A HIDEOUS
SHE-THING!
TERROR FROM THE YEAR 5,000
starring JOYCE HOLDEN · WARD COSTELLO · FREDERIC DOWNS
Produced, Directed and Written by ROBERT J. GURNEY • A JAMES H. NICHOLSON and SAMUEL Z. ARKOFF Production • AN AMERICAN-INTERNATIONAL PICTURE

## Terror from the Year 5,000

*UK title* Cage of Doom
*1958* American International
*Executive Producers* James H. Nicholson, Samuel Z. Arkoff
*Producer* Robert J. Gurney
*Director* Robert J. Gurney
*Screenplay* Robert J. Gurney
*Camera* Arthur Florman
*Editor* Dede Allen
*Art Director* Beatrice Gurney
74 minutes

Joyce Holden *Claire Erling*
Ward Costello *Robert Hedges*
Frederic Downs *Prof Erling*
John Stratton *Victor*
Fred Herrick *Angelo*
Beatrice Furdeaux *Miss Blake*
Jack Diamond *Technician*
Fred Taylor *Technician*
Salome Jens *The Woman*

Messrs James H. Nicholson and Samuel Z. Arkoff, prexy pair of the near-mighty American International Pictures, thought they had discovered another genius of the one-man movie-making talent of Roger Corman in young Robert J. Gurney, Junior. They were mistaken. This B-movie, or possibly C-movie, written, directed and produced by Junior, remains his testament, one that is very seldom seen today. Professor Erling builds a time machine in his laboratory, and successfully brings back a statuette which was made some centuries in the future. Unfortunately, it is radioactive. The prof's inquisitive assistant, John Stratton, has a dabble on his own when the prof isn't looking, and brings back a woman of tomorrow. Unfortunately she too turns out to be radioactive, a condition which has caused her some horrific disfiguration. She explains that in her world radioactivity has caused such havoc that all the babies are born deformed. What she needs to start a new, uncontaminated generation is some nice fresh pre-atomic genes, the very kind that keen young Stratton possesses. Stratton seems reluctant, so she hypnotises him into going forward into the future with her. Ward Costello, archaeologist, soon puts a stop to that by causing the time machine to disrupt, electrocuting both Stratton and the 'Hideous She-Thing' (quote, lobby card).

A WEIRD INVADER...TURNING OCEANS TO STEAM...MELTING MOUNTAINS...TURNING MEN AND WOMEN WHITE WITH THE AWESOME, HORRIBLE WAY IT KILLS!!!
YOU Won't Want To Look—But You Can't Help It!
YOU Won't Believe Your Eyes But—You'll Never Forget What They See!
YOU Won't Want To Stay—But You'll Be Glued To Your Seat!
WILLIAM BERKE PRODUCTIONS, INC. presents
THE LOST MISSILE
starring ROBERT LOGGIA · Larry Kerr · Ellen Parker · Philip Pine · Marilee Earle
with FRED ENGLEBERG · KITTY KELLY · SELMER JACKSON · Guest stars JOE HYAMS · BILL BRADLEY · Screenplay by JOHN McPARTLAND
and JEROME BIXBY · Based on a story by LESTER WILLIAM BERKE · Executive Producer WILLIAM BERKE · Produced by LEE GORDON
Directed by LESTER WILLIAM BERKE · Released thru UNITED UA ARTISTS

# The Lost Missile

*1958* William Berke Productions
*Distributor* United Artists
*Executive Producer* William Berke
*Producer* Lee Gordon
*Director* Lester William Berke
*Story* Lester William Berke
*Screenplay* John McPartland, Jerome Bixby
*Camera* Kenneth Peach
*Editor* Edward Sutherland
*Music* Gerald Fried
70 minutes

Robert Loggia *David Loring*
Larry Kerr *General Barr*
Ellen Parker *Joan Woods*
Philip Pine *Joe Freed*
Marilee Earle *Ella Freed*
Fred Engleberg *Personality*
Kitty Kelly *Mother*
Selmer Jackson *Secretary of State*
Joe Hyams *Young*
Bill Bradley *Brandley*

'A Weird Invader . . . Turning Oceans to Steam . . . Melting Mountains . . . Turning Men and Women White with the Awesome, Horrible Way it Kills!!!' In other words, those B-movie makers are cutting up the newsreel clips again. This time the cause is a missile from outer space running loose in the Earth's atmosphere, the heat of its velocity setting fire to cities and burning populations to a crisp. Ottawa is first to go, mainly because this film is a US-Canadian co-production, followed by others and elsewhere. Robert Loggia is the scientist who devises a makeshift means of destruction by screwing a spare hydrogen bomb warhead into a Nike missile, just in time to save Little Ole New York. The giant eye floating in space and the outsize clawing hand of the lobby card are examples of the publicist's art, and not to be confused with anything in the film itself! *The Lost Missile* was the final picture to be made by the late William Berke, a fact that might cause sighs among B-western movie aficionados.

THE Cosmic Man
AN ALLIED ARTISTS PICTURE Starring
BRUCE BENNETT JOHN CARRADINE
ANGELA GREENE SCOTTY MORROW
PRODUCED BY ROBERT A. TERRY
DIRECTED BY HERBERT GREENE
ORIGINAL STORY AND SCREENPLAY BY ARTHUR C. PIERCE

## *The Cosmic Man*

*1958* Future Productions
*Distributor* Allied Artists
*Producer* Robert A. Terry
*Director* Herbert Greene
*Screenplay* Arthur C. Pierce
*Camera* John F. Warren
*Music* Paul Sawtell, Bert Shefter
*Editors* Richard Currier, Helene Turner
*Special Effects* Charles Duncan
72 minutes

Bruce Bennett *Dr Karl Sorenson*
John Carradine *Cosmic Man*
Angela Greene *Kathy Grant*
Paul Langton *Col Matthews*
Scotty Morrow *Ken Grant*
Lyn Osborn *Sgt Gray*
Walter Marlow *Dr Richie*
Robert Lytton *Gen Knowland*

John Carradine, he of the lean and lanky look plus sinister sneer, arrives on Earth after a long career in low-budget vampire films, wearing a pair of dark sunglasses. This marks him as a mysterious alien, as if his arrival by outsize globular spaceship were not also a useful clue. Carradine becomes an instant target for Colonel Paul Langton and his military men, which upsets noble if not Nobel scientist, beefy Bruce Bennett, the former Tarzan of the Flicks. Blow up John Carradine and you blow up the landscape, he warns green-mindedly. Fortunately, Carradine, who is here on a goodwill mission despite all his weird appearance in double-exposure, cures poor little Scotty Morrow of crippleness and all ends more or less happily.

4D MAN
COLOR by DE LUXE
Starring
ROBERT LANSING
LEE MERIWETHER
and
JAMES CONGDON
Featuring
ROBERT STRAUSS · EDGAR STEHLI
Co-produced and Directed by
IRVIN SHORTESS YEAWORTH, JR.
Screenplay by
THEODORE SIMONSON and CY CHERMAK
Produced by
JACK H. HARRIS
A FAIRVIEW PRODUCTION
A UNIVERSAL-INTERNATIONAL RELEASE

# 4D Man

*also titled* Master of Terror; The Evil Force
*1959* Fairview Productions
*Distributor* Universal-International
*Producers* Jack H. Harris,
Irvin Shortess Yeaworth Jr
*Director* Irvin Shortess Yeaworth Jr
*Story* Jack H. Harris
*Screenplay* Theodore Simsonson,
Cy Chermak
*Camera* Theodore J. Pahle
*Special Effects* Barton Sloan
*Editor* William Murphy
*Music* Ralph Carmichael
85 minutes DeLuxe Color

Robert Lansing *Scott Nelson*
Lee Meriwether *Linda Davis*
James Congdon *Tony Nelson*
Robert Strauss *Roy Parker*
Edgar Stehli *Carson*
Patty Duke
Jasper Deeter

At the time this was shown, the title would have meant *The Fourpenny Man* to British audiences, and thus it was changed to *Master of Terror*, and again to *The Evil Force*. Not that this helped much at the box-office, where the actors' names were virtually meaningless, even in America. The film was shot at the Valley Forge Studios, Pennsylvania, which may account for it – or may not. '4D' is, in this instance, initialese for the Fourth Dimension, a status that occurs to research scientist Robert Lansing in his search for some way to penetrate matter. The process backfires on him, leaving him able to walk through walls. Unfortunately, the electrical effect on his brainwaves begins to use up his Life Force at an alarming rate, and he needs must extract this mysterious substance from others in order to replenish his system. A process which, naturally, leads to their death. As his own premature ageing accelerates, the white-haired and wrinkled young scientist finds his fourth-dimensional powers waning ever more rapidly, until one day they vanish whilst he is actually on the job, and he winds up as part of the foundations of the new building next door. Pity nobody was around to murmur the obvious obituary: 'Pity about Dr Nelson – he was a brick'.

BATTLE
IN OUTER
SPACE
IN EASTMAN
COLOR
Filmed in TOHOSCOPE · A TOHO PRODUCTION
A COLUMBIA PICTURES RELEASE

# Battle in Outer Space

*Original title* Uchu Daisenso
*1959* Toho Productions
*Distributor* Columbia Pictures
*Producer* Tomoyuki Tanaka
*Director* Inoshiro Honda
*Story* Jotaro Okami
*Screenplay* Shinichi Sekizawa
*Camera* Hajime Koizumi
*Special Effects* Eiji Tsuburaya
*Editor* Kazuji Taira
*Art Director* Teruaki Ando
*Music* Akira Hukube
93 minutes Eastmancolor Tohoscope

Ryo Ikebe *Dr Katsumiya*
Kyoko Anzai *Dr Etsuko*
Minoru Takada
Koreya Senda
Len Stanford
Harold Conway
George Whitman
Elise Richter
Hisaya Ito
Yoshio Tsuchiya
Hiro-O Kirino
Kozo Nomura
Fuyuki Murakami
Leonard Walsh

Set a few years ahead (in 1965), this Toho epic in Tohoscope forsakes the usual obligatory razing of Tokyo for the destruction of Venice (by flood), New York (by fire), and the Golden Gate Bridge of San Francisco (by Space Torpedo). Fiends to blame for this decimation of Earth are an invasion force of outer space aliens parked on the far side of the moon. To carry out their interplanetary plot they implant tiny transistors in the brains of a pair of Japanese astronauts, who zap back to the home space-base and start all the trouble. Soon the United Nations (minus the Union of Soviet Socialist Republics) strike back and bang goes the lunar Sea of Tranquillity. A field day for Special Effects expert Eiji Tsuburaya, if not for the actors and those who dubbed them.

CALTIKI
The Immortal Monster
with
JOHN MERIVALE · DIDI SULLIVAN · GERARD HERTER
DANIELA ROCCA DIRECTED BY ROBERT HAMTON
SCREENPLAY BY PHILLIP JUST A SAMUEL SCHNEIDER Presentation
PRODUCTION BY CLIMAX PICTURES — GALATEA Distribution by Lux Film AN ALLIED ARTISTS PICTURE

# *Caltiki the Immortal Monster*

*Original title* Caltiki il Mostro Immortale
*1959* Galatea/Climax/Lux
*Distributor* Allied Artists
*Producer* Samuel Schneider
*Director* Robert Hamton (Ricardo Freda)
*Screenplay* Philip Just (Filippano Sanjust)
*Camera* John Foam (Mario Bava)
*Editor* Salvatore Billiterri
76 minutes

John Merivale *Prof John Fielding*
Didi Sullivan *Ellen*
Gerard Herter *Max*
Daniela Rocca *Linda*
Daniele Pitani *Bob*
Gay Pearl *Dancer*

Set in Mexico, this Italian-made monstrosity succeeded in fooling Americans into thinking it was home-made, thanks to the Yankee-isation of the names of the main film-makers, and the casting of minor British B-player John Merivale in the leading role. He played scientist John Fielding leading a team of archaeologists in search of a Mayan tomb. They find it, and in it they also find Caltiki, a long-lost local God. After destroying the big blob in a battle royal, they take a bit back to the lab, always a fatal thing to do. It promptly begins to revive and renew itself, and soon is enlarging and expanding all over the place. Fortunately, one of the scientists succeeds in translating a fragment of mysterious Mayan writing found close to the tomb, and they learn that the coming of a comet will bestow upon Caltiki a dose of immortal life. And what do you know, a comet is currently on the way! By dint of applying fire, Caltiki is destroyed again, just in time.

Just what was Caltiki made of? Mario Bava, the film's cameraman and later director of many a Spaghetti Western, explained: 'It was a ton of cow's entrails with a man hidden inside to make it move'. His biggest problem? 'Keeping the flies away!'

THE
ATOMIC SUBMARINE
AN ALLIED ARTISTS PICTURE
starring ARTHUR FRANZ · DICK FORAN
BRETT HALSEY With JOI LANSING · PAUL DUBOV
BOB STEELE · VICTOR VARCONI and TOM CONWAY
as Sir Ian Hunt

# The Atomic Submarine

*1959* Gorham Productions
*Distributor* Allied Artists
*Producer* Alex Gordon
*Associate Producer* Orville H. Hampton
*Co-Producer* Henry Schrage
*Director* Spencer Gordon Bennet
*Story* Jack Rabin, Irving Block
*Screenplay* Orville H. Hampton
*Camera* Gilbert Warrenton
*Special Effects* Jack Rabin, Irving Block, Louis DeWitt
*Music* Alexander Laszlo
*Art Directors* Don Ament, Daniel Haller
*Editor* William Austin
72 minutes

Arthur Franz *Commodore Reef Holloway*
Dick Foran *Capt Dan Wendover*
Brett Halsey *Carl Nelson*
Joi Lansing *Julie*
Paul Dubov *Lt David Milton*
Bob Steele *Griff*
Victor Varconi *Dr Clifford Kent*
Tom Conway *Sir Ian Hunt*
Selmer Jackson *Admiral Terhune*
Jack Mulhall *Murdock*
Jean Moorhead *Helen*
Richard Tyler *Carney*
Sid Melton *Chester*
Ken Becker *Powell*
Pat Michaels *Narrator*

A curious crew of former B-movie stars (Dick Foran, Tom Conway, Bob Steele, Victor Varconi, Jack Mulhall) board an atomic-powered United States Navy submarine, sent to seek out the reason for a series of suspicious disasters 'neath the North Pole. Much to their, but not our, surprise they locate a Flying Saucer from outer space swimming about underneath the ice-cap. And much to everybody's surprise, the entire UFO turns out to be nothing less than a living alien organism! This outsized one-eyed oddity is fashioned from seaweed and suchlike by the Special Effects team of Jack Rabin and Irving Block, who also wrote the original story! A nearby nuclear warhead soon stops its game.

LAND ON THE MOON WITH THE
FIRST INTREPID ASTRONAUTS!
12 TO THE MOON
starring
AN INTERNATIONAL CAST
Screenplay by DeWITT BODEEN
Story by FRED GEBHARDT · Directed by DAVID BRADLEY · Produced by FRED GEBHARDT
A COLUMBIA
PICTURES
RELEASE

# 12 to the Moon

*1960* Luna Productions
*Distributor* Columbia
*Producer* Fred Gebhardt
*Director* David Bradley
*Screenplay* DeWitt Bodeen
*Camera* John Alton
*Special Effects* Howard Anderson, E. Nicholson
*Art Director* Rudi Feld
*Editor* Edward Mann
*Music* Michael Anderson
74 minutes

Ken Clark *Capt John Anderson*
Anthony Dexter *Dr Luis Vargas*
Robert Montgomery Jr *Roddy Murdoch*
Tom Conway *Dr Feodor Orloff*
John Wengraf *Dr Erik Heinrich*
Cory Devlin *Dr Asmara Makonen*
Tema Bey *Dr Selim Hamid*
Anna Lisa *Dr Sigrid Bromark*
Michi Kobi *Dr Hideo Murata*
Roger Till *Dr Etienne Martel*
Richard Weber *Dr David Ruskin*
Philip Baird *Dr Rochester*
Francis X. Bushman *Narrator*

'Starring an International Cast!' cried the lobby-cards. 'Name us!' screamed the actors, 'or we won't go!' Very well, but not all twelve, ten of whom were doctors – enough for several telly soap-operas. There was Ken Clark, the Captain (who?); Tom Conway (ah yes, the Falcon's brother!); Anthony Dexter (not that chap who played Rudolph Valentino again?); Robert Montgomery Junior (son of you know who); and Francis X. Bushman, hot from his success in the original silent version of *Ben Hur*. On the other side of the camera there was David Bradley, who usually directed *Pete Smith Specialities*, and DeWitt Bodeen, sophisticated scriptwriter of *Cat People*. A gathering of international scientists climbs aboard the Lunar Eagle One for a peaceful probe. Unfortunately, deep beneath the crater Menelaus lurks the Great Coordinator, ruler of the moon. In return for this unwarranted disturbance of his lifestyle, the Coordinator enveloped the Earth in a cold white cloud, intending to freeze our planet into oblivion. Our gang rocket back home and drop an atomic bomb into a Mexican volcano, the ideal plan for warming us up again. Pity it fails.

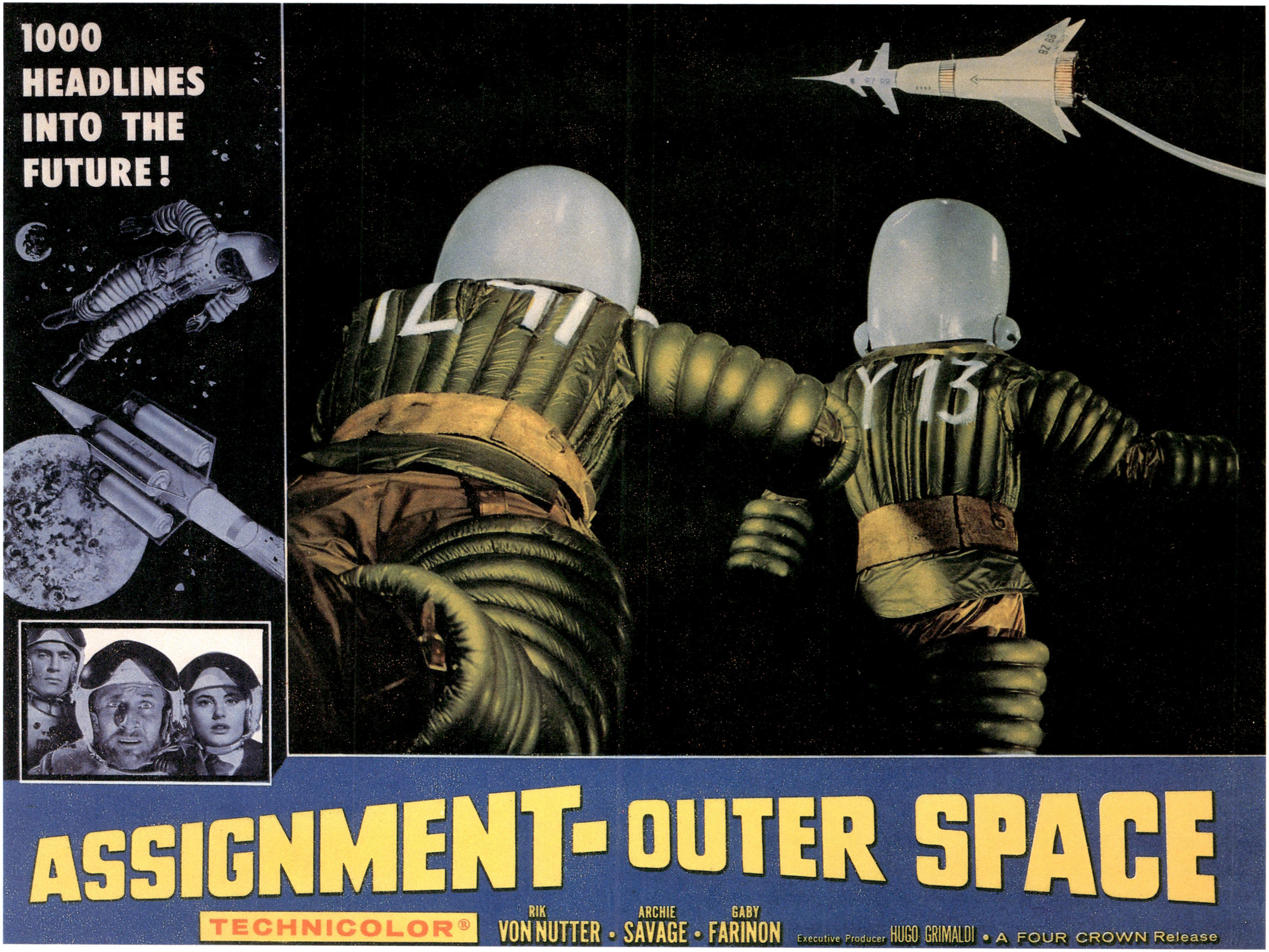
1000 HEADLINES INTO THE FUTURE!
ASSIGNMENT- OUTER SPACE
TECHNICOLOR®
RIK VON NUTTER · ARCHIE SAVAGE · GABY FARINON
Executive Producer HUGO GRIMALDI • A FOUR CROWN Release

# Assignment – Outer Space

*Original title* Space Men
*1960* Italy/Ultra Films/Titanus
*Distributor* Four Crown Productions
*Producer* Hugo Grimaldi
*Director* Antonio Margheriti
*Story* Vassily Petrov
*Camera* Marcello Maciocchi
*Special Effects* Caesar Peace
*Music* J.K. Broady; Gordon Zahler (US)
73 minutes Technicolor

Rik Von Nutter *Ray Peterson*
Gaby (Gabriella) Farinon *Lucy*
Archie Savage
David Montressor
Alain Dijon
Franco Fantasia

This Italian science-fiction spectacular was the first of a run of seven to be directed by Antonio Margheriti, better known in English-speaking circles as Anthony Dawson.

Rik Von Nutter played journalist Ray Peterson on a visit to an orbiting space station, sometime in the future. With his loved one, Lucy (Gaby Farinon), he heads into outer space to save the Earth from a runaway rocketship which is under the erratic control of an electronic brain.

'One Thousand Headlines into the Future!' shrieked the lobby cards, carefully concealing all traces of the film's foreign origins.

ROBUR THE CONQUEROR
AND HIS AMAZING
FLYING WARSHIP...
DESTROYER OF THE ARMIES
AND THE NAVIES OF THE
WORLD...THE FABULOUS
ADVENTURES OF THE MAN
WHO CONQUERED THE
EARTH TO SAVE IT!
AMERICAN-INTERNATIONAL presents
JULES VERNE'S
MASTER OF THE WORLD
starring VINCENT PRICE · CHARLES BRONSON · HENRY HULL · MARY WEBSTER · DAVID FRANKHAM
Directed by WILLIAM WITNEY · Produced by JAMES H. NICHOLSON · Screenplay by RICHARD MATHESON · Music by LES BAXTER
IN MAGNACOLOR

# Master of the World

*1961* American-International
*Producer* James H. Nicholson
*Director* William Witney
*Story* from the novels *Master of the World* and *Robur the Conqueror* by Jules Verne
*Screenplay* Richard Matheson
*Camera* Gil Warrenton
*Special Effects* Ray Mercer, Tim Barr, Wah Chang, Gene Warren
*Art Director* Daniel Haller
*Editor* Anthony Carras
*Music* Les Baxter
104 minutes Magnacolor

Vincent Price *Robur*
Charles Bronson *Strock*
Henry Hull *Prudent*
Mary Webster *Dorothy*
David Frankham *Philip*
Richard Harrison *Alistair*
Vito Scotti *Topage*
Wally Campo *Turner*
Steve Masino *Weaver*
Ken Terrell *Shanks*
Peter Besbas *Wilson*

Jules Verne, the French master of early science-fiction (in the days when it was called *Voyages Imaginaires)* wrote his famous novel, *Clipper of the Clouds,* in 1886, and its sequel, *Master of the World,* some eighteen years later. He also wrote *Robur the Conqueror,* and while two of these three books are credited with being the source for this epic, American write-ups are at variance from the British. Whichever were the origins, it was the American author of many short stories in the fantasy genre, Richard Matheson, who hammered out this screenplay, one of many he wrote for American-International Pictures at this time. He set his version in 1848, and AIP's favourite fantasy star, Vincent Price, usually to be seen amidst the cobwebby crypts and creeperies of Edgar Allan Poe, was cast as Robur the Conqueror. As a not too distant relation to Verne's other megalamaniac millionaire, Captain Nemo, Robur swoops through the Victorian skyscapes in his multi-propellered dirigible, *The Albatross,* intent on ending for all time the scourge of warfare by destroying the world's armies and navies. Or, as the lobby-card put it, 'The Adventures of the Man who Conquered the Earth to Save it!' He fails, of course.

SPACE TRAVELERS IN A WORLD THAT TIME FORGOT!
VALLEY OF THE DRAGONS
Mastodons! Dinosaurs! Flying Reptiles! Humankind makes its last stand!
Battle for survival-- Against brutal, bestial Neanderthals!
Subterranean mole-men inflicting weird tortures on all captives!
in MONSTASCOPE
starring
CESARE DANOVA · SEAN McCLORY · JOAN STALEY
Screenplay by EDWARD BERNDS · Story by DONALD ZIMBALIST · Based on a story by JULES VERNE
Produced by BYRON ROBERTS · Executive Producer, ALFRED ZIMBALIST · Directed by EDWARD BERNDS
A ZRB PRODUCTION · A COLUMBIA PICTURES RELEASE

# Valley of the Dragons

*1961* Z.R.B. Productions
*Distributor* Columbia
*Executive Producer* Alfred Zimbalist
*Producer* Byron Roberts
*Director* Edward Bernds
*Story* from the novel *Career of a Comet* by Jules Verne
*Adaptation* Donald Zimbalist
*Screenplay* Edward Bernds
*Camera* Brydon Baker
*Special Effects* Dick Albain
*Editor* Edwin Bryant
*Music* Ruby Raksin
79 minutes Monstascope

Cesare Danova *Hector Servadac*
Sean McClory *Denning*
Joan Staley *Deena*
Danielle De Metz *Nateeta*
Gregg Martell *Odloo*
Gil Perkins *Tarn*
I. Stanford Jolley *Patoo*
Michael Lane *Aooka*
Roger Till *Vidal*
Mark Dempsey *Andrews*
Jerry Sunshine *Le Clerc*
Dolly Gray *Mara*

'Space Travelers in a World that Time Forgot!' shrieked the lobby cards. 'Mastodons! Dinosaurs! Flying Reptiles! Humankind makes its Last Stand!' *Variety*, the trade paper for film folk, created a new portmaneau word for this little glue-and-new epic: they called it an 'iguanachronism'! Alfred Zimbalist produced it from a script by young Donald Zimbalist, making it a truly family film. In his turn, the junior Zimbalist based his stuff on an old Jules Verne novel from the Nineties, *Career of a Comet*, aka *Off on a Comet*, aka *Hector Servadac*. Plus, of course, a pile of that popular stock footage from 1939's *One Million BC*. Of such things are new movies made. The year is 1881 when a straying celestial comet swipes Earth, sweeping a chunk into space upon which are our two heroes, Hector and Denning. Once in steady orbit, the two of them meet not only Hal Roach's gang of dinosaurs, but a beauteous brace of Mesozoic maidens called Deena and Nateeta. Prehistoric life is clearly not all that bad, especially when the adventurers have not only the civilizing effects of gunpowder, but also petting to demonstrate to the natives.

WHAT IS THIS MONSTROUS THING?
With the power of mind over matter!... There beyond the stars your unspeakable fears... deepest desires... come alive ...and you are trapped in a spectacle of terror—your secret fears pitted against you!
Journey to the Seventh planet
in color
STARRING JOHN AGAR · GRETA THYSSEN · ANN SMYRNER · MIMI HEINRICH
screenplay by SIDNEY PINK and IB MELCHOIR · produced and directed by SIDNEY PINK · a CINEMAGIC production · an AMERICAN INTERNATIONAL PICTURE

## Journey to the Seventh Planet

*1961* Cinemagic Productions
*Distributor* American International
*Producer* Sidney Pink
*Director* Sidney Pink
*Story* Sidney Pink
*Screenplay* Sidney Pink, Ib Melchior
*Camera* Age Wiltrup
*Special Effects* Bent Barford
*Music* Ib Glindemann
78 minutes colour

John Agar *Don*
Greta Thyssen *Greta*
Ann Smyrner *Ingrid*
Mimi Heinrich *Ursula*
Carl Ottoson *Eric*
Ove Sprogoe *Harry*
Louis Renard *Svend*
Peter Monch *Karl*
Annie Garde *Ellen*
Ulla Moritz *Lise*
Bente Juel *Colleen*

That John Agar certainly gets around. Here he is on the planet Uranus in the year 2001, captaining a United Nations crew of explorers. The green planet seems uninhabited until one of the gang, a chap scared of rats, is attacked by a giant rodent. Next, a homesick Swede finds himself in a replica of his village, and before you can say Jill Robinson, all the men meet delicious images of their hometown girlfriends. Or, as the lobby card writer put it, 'There beyond the stars your unspeakable fears . . . deepest desires . . . come alive . . . and you are trapped in a spectacle of terror, your secret fears pitted against you!' The spacemen realise that their brain patterns are being read to produce these strange effects by the sole occupant of Uranus, a giant globule not unlike an eyeball. The idea is to drive the intruders away. However, being led by John Agar, they devise a cunning method of destroying the creature by subjecting it to ultra-low temperature via liquid oxygen. Thus is Uranus made safe for Earthfolks.

ASSOCIATED PRODUCERS INC. presents
HAND OF DEATH
3061
Released by 20 Century-Fox
starring JOHN AGAR · PAULA RAYMOND · STEVE DUNNE
Written and Produced by EUGENE LING · Directed by GENE NELSON

## *Hand of Death*

*1962* Associated Producers
*Distributor* Twentieth Century-Fox
*Producer* Eugene Ling
*Director* Gene Nelson
*Screenplay* Eugene Ling
*Camera* Floyd Crosby
*Editor* Carl Pierson
*Art Director* Harry Reif
*Music* Sonny Burke
*Makeup* Bob Mark
59 minutes CinemaScope

John Agar *Dr Alex Marsh*
Paula Raymond *Carol Wilson*
Steve Dunne *Tom Holland*
Roy Gordon *Dr Ramsey*
John Alonzo *Carlos*

Here comes genial John Agar again, this time thicker than usual: his skin thickens and cracks up like some hippopotamus with galloping acne. He plays scientist Alex Marsh, working at one of those lone laboratories out in the American desert. He is experimenting with a dangerous new gas when an accident brings him into contact with the stuff. Soon his skin turns tanned, a little too deeply to be termed fashionable. He grasps the arm of his assistant, Carlos, and the man promptly drops dead on the spot. He bears the marks of a first-degree burn where the doc's hand touched him! Marsh does the only thing possible: he sets fire to the laboratory. By the time he has reached the home of his boss, Dr Ramsey, his skin has turned black. A thoughtless touch, and Ramsey, too, drops down dead. By now Marsh has become truly thick-skinned and all that remains is for the police to corner him on the beach and mow him down.

What a curious film for dancing Gene Nelson to direct.

SCIENCE SHOCKER
OF THE SPACE AGE!
THE
PHANTOM PLANET
DEAN FREDERICKS · COLEEN GRAY · TONY DEXTER
And Introducing DOLORES FAITH
Produced by FRED GEBHARDT · Directed by WILLIAM MARSHALL · Screen Story by FRED GEBHARDT
A FOUR CROWN Production

# The Phantom Planet

*1962* Four Crown Productions
*Executive Producer* Leo Handel
*Producer* Fred Gebhardt
*Director* William Marshall
*Screenplay* Fred Gebhardt
*Camera* Elwood Nicholson
*Editor* Hugo Grimaldi
*Art Director* Bob Kinoshita
*Music* Hayes Pagel
82 minutes

Dean Fredericks *Capt Frank Chapman*
Coleen Gray *Liara*
Tony Dexter *Herron*
Dolores Faith *Zetha*
Francis X. Bushman *Seson*
Richard Weber *Lt Makonnen*
Al Jarvis *Judge Eden*
Dick Haynes *Col Lansfield*
Earl McDaniel *Pilot Leonard*
Michael Marshall *Lt White*
John Herrin *Capt Beecher*
Mel Curtis *Lt Cutler*
Jimmy Weldon *Webb*
Akemi Tani *Officer*
Lori Lyons *Radar Officer*
Richard Kiel *Solarite*

Hard to credit that the co-pilot of this expedition into outer space was none other than Anthony Dexter, once the portrayer of Hollywood's Greatest Lover of the silent screen, Rudolph Valentino. But such is life in Tinseltown, and soon Dexter's spaceship, the *Pegasus Four*, is badly damaged by a storm of meteorites whilst on a mission to investigate the disappearance of a previous probe. The astronauts attempt a repair whilst drifting in space, but are forced to land on a handy asteroid. They discover the atmosphere is breathable, but are surprised to find it has an unexpected property – it causes them to shrink! This whittles them down to the same size as the rest of the population, who proceed to capture them. When a rival faction steals one of their leading ladies, the attractive but mute Zetha, the Captain saves her and then defends the little folk against their startlingly oversized enemy, a cannibalistic monstrosity played to the hilt of his super shoulder-pads by Richard *(Jaws)* Keil. Having duly dispensed of the creature, the Captain climbs into his spacesuit, returns to normal size, and heads for home – but will anybody believe his story? Would you?

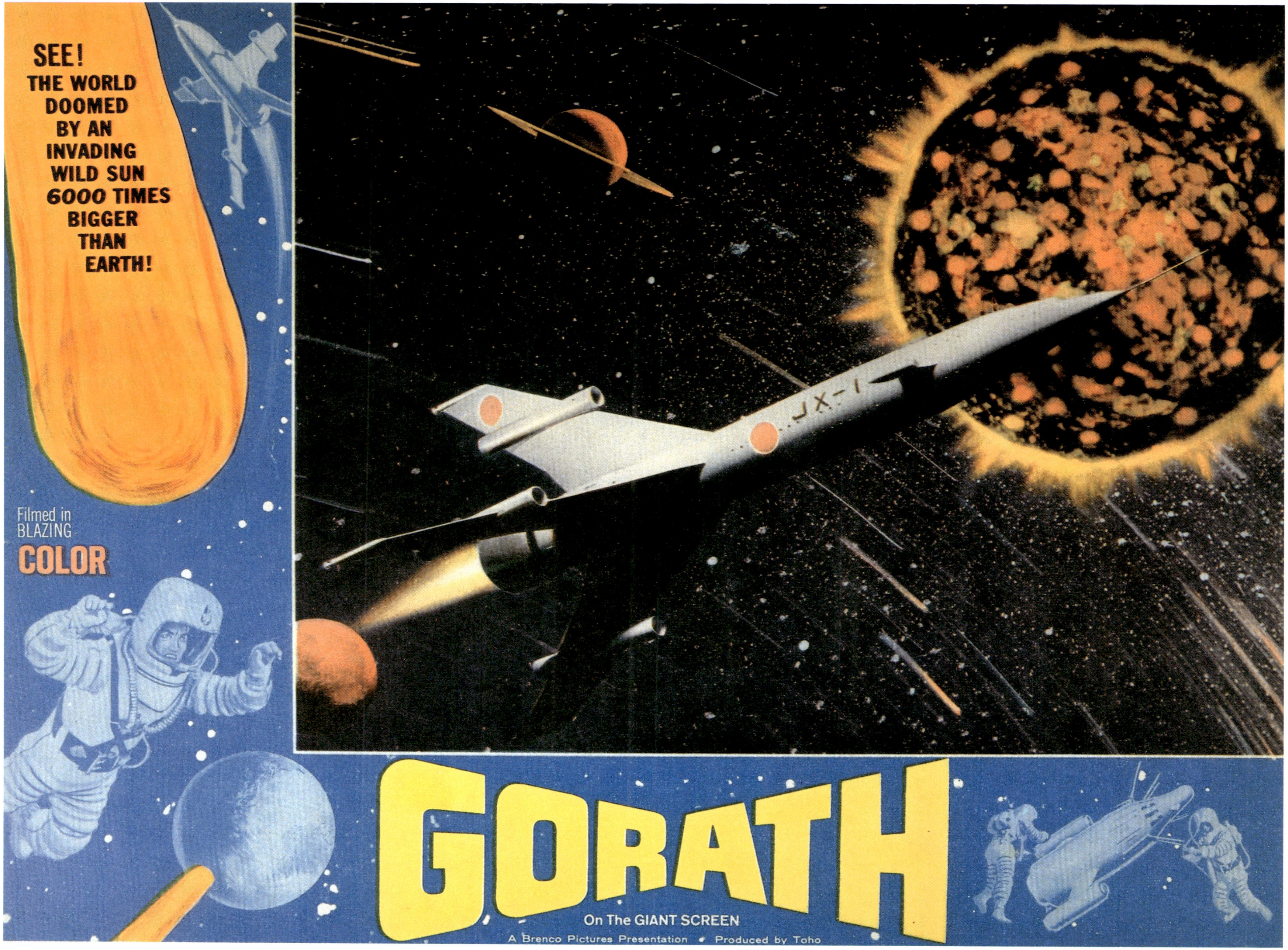

SEE!
THE WORLD DOOMED BY AN INVADING WILD SUN 6000 TIMES BIGGER THAN EARTH!
Filmed in BLAZING COLOR
JX-1
GORATH
On The GIANT SCREEN
A Brenco Pictures Presentation • Produced by Toho

# Gorath

*Original title* Yosei Gorasu
*1962* Toho
*Distributor* Brenco Pictures
*Producer* Tomoyuki Tanaka
*Director* Inoshiro Honda
*Screenplay* Takeshi Kimura
*Camera* Hajime Koizumi
*Special Effects* Eiji Tsuburaya
*Music* Kan Ishil
89 minutes Eastmancolor Tohoscope

Ryo Ikebe
Akihiko Hirata
Jun Tazaki
Yumi Shirakawa
Takashi Shimura
Kumi Mizuno

What would you do if you learned that 'an invading wild sun six thousand times bigger than Earth' was rushing headlong in your direction? So would I – but here is what the Japanese did about it. They made a movie, in Blazing Color, of course, and the very wide screen of Tohoscope . Famed oriental director Inoshiro Honda entitled his film *Yosei Gorasu,* but the American outfit, Brenco Pictures Corporation, run by veteran flicker folk Edward L. Alperson and Stanley Meyer, preferred the more pronounceable *Gorath.* An international but remarkably Japanese-looking group of scientists discover that a runaway planet is on a collision course for Earth. They send up a spaceship to investigate, and it manages to radio back some useful information on the unheavenly body before crashing into the fiery surface. A solution is finally found. A rack of rockets is embedded into the South Pole and ignited, thus pushing the Earth out of its orbit to let the celestial invader fly by. Unfortunately, the resulting earthquake unleashes a further horror, a monstrous prehistoric walrus. This the Japanese with their gift for language promptly christen Gorath, and once again Tokyo is under strenuous siege.

JOLTING SPACE SHOCKER!
The CRAWLING HAND
ASTRONAUT ORDERED BLOWN-UP! TERRIFYING MENACE FROM MOON
She revealed her body, but not the secret.
VIOLENT MURDER
JOSEPH F. ROBERTSON'S The
CRAWLING HAND

# The Crawling Hand

*1963* Hansen Enterprises
*Producer* Joseph F. Robertson
*Director* Herbert L. Strock
*Story* Robert Young, Joseph Cranston
*Screenplay* Herbert L. Strock, William Edelson
*Camera* Willard Van Der Veer
*Editor* Herbert L. Strock
89 minutes

Peter Breck *Steve Curan*
Kent Taylor *Doc Weitzberg*
Rod Lauren *Paul Laurence*
Sirry Steffen *Marta Farnstrom*
Alan Hale (Jr) *Sheriff*
Arline Judge *Mrs Hotchkiss*
Richard Arlen
Alison Hayes

A choice of sensation was offered by the lobby card for this minor but overlong epic: 'Jolting Space Shocker!' or 'She Revealed Her Body but Not Her Secret!' None of the cast made it to the publicity, however, which seems odd as the roster of former B-movie stalwarts is impressive. All had been box-office back in the Forties in the heydays of Monogram and PRC. The screenplay, owing much to *The Beast With Five Fingers*, concerns a severed hand with a life of its own. This becomes animatedly detached from its owner when an astronaut returns to Earth and his spaceship explodes. Medical student Rod Lauren finds the missing member and takes it home, where it promptly strangles his landlady. Lauren pockets the hand and becomes infected with its powers. Not only does he have the desire to strangle strangers, but he also goes a little dark around the eyes. Finally the hand from outer space is defeated in a way unique in the movies. A passing cat eats it for lunch.

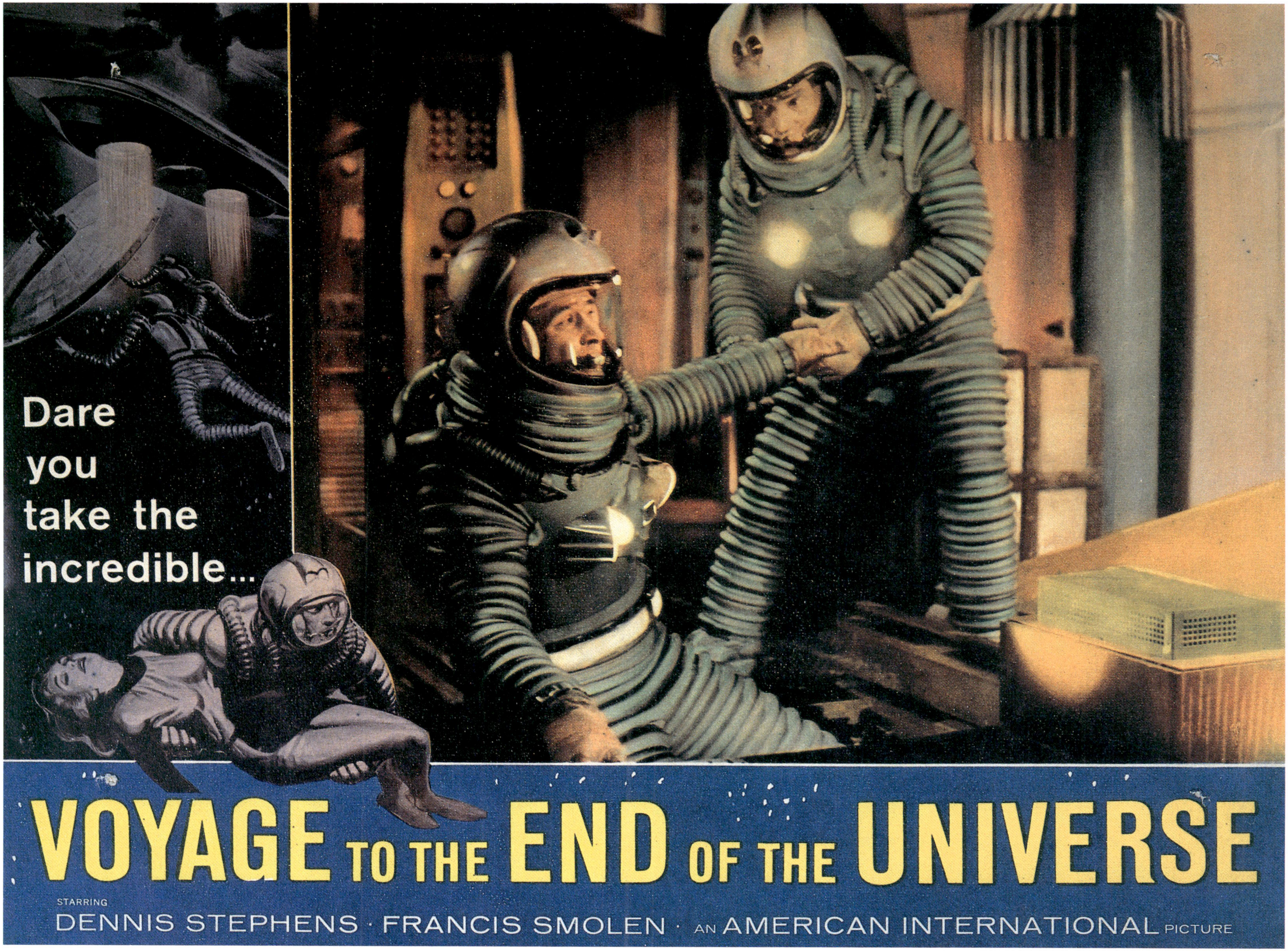
Dare
you
take the
incredible...
VOYAGE TO THE END OF THE UNIVERSE
STARRING
DENNIS STEPHENS · FRANCIS SMOLEN · AN AMERICAN INTERNATIONAL PICTURE

## *Voyage to the End of the Universe*

*Original title* Ikarie XB – 1
*1963* Czechoslovak State Films
*Distributor* American International
*Producer* Rudolph Wohl
*Director* Jindrich Polak
*Screenplay* Pavel Juracek, Indrich Polak
*Camera* Jan Kalis
*Editor* Josef Dubricovsky
65 (90) minutes

Dennis Stephens *Vladimir*
(Zdenek Stepanek)
Francis Smolen *Anthony*
(Frantisek Smolik)
Radovan Lukavsky *MacDonald*
Dana Medricka *Nina*
Miroslav Machacek *Marcel*
Jiri Vrstala *Erik*

'Dare You Take the Incredible Voyage to the End of the Universe?' demanded the lobby cards? If you took the American version of the trip, it would only have taken you 65 minutes, instead of the full ninety of the original picture. For this was a Czechoslovakian film, although you would never have known it by the American International Pictures release. They not only changed the names of the stars so they could bill a couple of semi-American names, they also, perhaps, added the grand finale when the space travellers touch down on the Green Planet – and spot the Statue of Liberty! The year is sometime in the 25th century, and a large spaceship blasts off bearing forty people on a long trip to a faraway Green Planet. Many adventures befall them. A radiating star induces the crew to doze dangerously off. A derelict spaceship is encountered, boarded, and found to be some centuries old. Live atomic bombs are found, which cause accidental death to the travellers. Meanwhile a baby is born aboard, somebody goes mad from claustrophobia, and so on until their destination is reached, and the ship touches down. Highly polished stuff, including the gleaming interiors.

One U. S. astronaut
pitted against all the odds
beyond this earth!
ROBINSON CRUSOE
ON MARS
TECHNICOLOR
THIS FILM IS
SCIENTIFICALLY
AUTHENTIC
...IT IS ONLY ONE STEP
AHEAD OF PRESENT
REALITY!

# Robinson Crusoe on Mars

*1964* Devonshire Pictures
*Distributor* Paramount Pictures
*Producer* Aubrey Schenck
*Director* Byron Haskin
*Story* fom the novel *Robinson Crusoe* by Daniel Defoe
*Screenplay* Ib Melchior, John C. Higgins
*Camera* Winton Hoch
*Special Effects* Laurence Butler
*Art Director* Hal Periera
*Music* Van Cleve
*Editor* Terry Morse
*Makeup* Wally Westmore
110 minutes Technicolor

Paul Mantee *Cdr Christopher Draper*
Victor Lundin *Friday*
Mona the Monkey
Adam West *Col Dan McReady*

Starring a named cast of three – Paul Mantee, Victor Lundin and Mona the Woolly Monkey – this mini-epic (although at a running-time of almost two hours, the term 'mini' scarcely seems to apply) also featured a mini-moment with Adam West, who in due course would become TV's *Batman*. Here he is killed right at the start, while Mantee goes on to crashland successfully on the planet Mars. His ejector capsule also carried Mona the Woolly Monkey, so Mantee is not exactly a lone Crusoe. The picture takes its plotline from the 250-year-old novel by Daniel Defoe, yet still manages to live up to its lobby card line, 'This Film is Scientifically Authentic – it is Only One Step Ahead of Present Reality!' Well, almost. Bit by bit, man and monkey learn to live in their rough new environment. Then one day a tall slave escapes from his captors, and becomes Mantee's somewhat servile companion. Mantee promptly names him 'Friday'! The slave's alien captors go to great extremes to grab him back, bombarding Mars with all manner of explosive rays, but the trio manage to escape through some subterranean tunnels to the Martian icecap, where they are saved by a US spaceship. Death Valley stood in for the Martian landscape, by the way.

YOU are in the FUTURE before it happens!
AMERICAN INTERNATIONAL PRESENTS
THE TIME TRAVELERS IN COLOR
STARRING PRESTON FOSTER · PHILIP CAREY · MERRY ANDERS · JOHN HOYT · FEATURING DENNIS PATRICK · MUSIC BY RICHARD LA SALLE · SCREENPLAY BY IB MELCHIOR · STORY BY DAVID HEWITT & IB MELCHIOR · PRODUCED BY WILLIAM REDLIN · DIRECTED BY IB MELCHIOR · A DOBIL PRODUCTION

# The Time Travellers

*1964* Dobil Productions
*Distributor* American International
*Producer* William Redlin
*Director* Ib Melchior
*Story* Ib Melchior, David Hewitt
*Screenplay* Ib Melchior
*Camera* William Zsigmond
*Special Effects* David Hewitt
*Editor* Hal Dennis
*Art Director* Ray Storey
*Music* Richard La Salle
84 minutes Pathecolor

Preston Foster *Dr Erik von Steiner*
Philip Carey *Steve Connors*
Merry Anders *Carol White*
John Hoyt *Varno*
Dennis Patrick *Councillor Willard*
Joan Woodbury *Gadra*
Dolores Wells *Reena*
Steve Franken *Danny McKee*
Gloria Leslie *Council woman*
Peter Strudwick *Deviant*
Margaret Seldeen *Technician*
Forrest J. Ackerman *Third Technician*

'You Are in the Future Before It Happens!' cried the lobby cards. Especially if you are B-picture stalwarts Preston Foster and Phil Carey. They played a pair of profs on a college campus who constructed a Time Warp Space Portal – or was it a Space Warp Time Portal? Whichever, it works, and they, plus the obligatory pretty girl (Merry Anders) and the equally obligatory comedy relief (Steve Franken – remember him as the drunken waiter in *The Party*?) are whisked through the gateway to tomorrow, landing dazedly in the year 2071. They are oddly surprised to find the Earth has been desolated by dint of a disastrous nuclear war, another obligatory item in Sixties cinematic sci-fi. The human inhabitants seem much the same as those of '64, save that they bear names like Varno, Gadra and Reena. They live underground, while overground are the dreadedly hideous Mutants. Serving the survivors are the Androids, robots constructed by Technicians, one of whom (the third) is played by Surprise Guest Star Forrest J. Ackerman, editor of *Famous Monsters of Filmland!* The plan afoot is to build a spaceship to fly the decent folks to the nearest star, but our heroes opt to return to their time. They misjudge the dials while one of the party gets trapped in a perpetual time cycle. Poor sod.

THE DAY THE EARTH SPLIT IN TWO!
TODAY'S TERRIFYING LOOK INTO WHAT MIGHT HAPPEN TOMORROW
CRACK IN THE WORLD
TECHNICOLOR
Starring DANA ANDREWS · JANETTE SCOTT · KIERON MOORE · ALEXANDER KNOX
PRODUCED BY BERNARD GLASSER AND LESTER A. SANSOM · DIRECTED BY ANDREW MARTON
A PARAMOUNT RELEASE
SCREENPLAY BY JON MANCHIP WHITE AND JULIAN HALEVY · STORY BY JON MANCHIP WHITE · EXECUTIVE PRODUCER PHILIP YORDAN

## *Crack in the World*

*1964* Security Pictures
*Distributor* Paramount
*Executive Producer* Philip Yordan
*Producers* Bernard Glasser, Lester A. Sansom
*Director* Andrew Marton
*Story* Jon Manchip White
*Screenplay* Jon Manchip White, Julian Halevy
*Camera* Manuel Berenguer
*Special Effects* Alec Weldon
*Editor* Derek Parsons
*Music* John Douglas
*Art Director* Eugene Lourie
96 minutes Technicolor

Dana Andrews *Dr Stephen Sorenson*
Janette Scott *Maggie Sorenson*
Kieron Moore *Ted Rampion*
Alexander Knox *Sir Charles Eggerston*
Peter Damon *Masefield*
Gary Lasdun *Markov*
Mike Steen *Steele*
Todd Martin *Simpson*
Jim Gillen *Rand*

'The Day the Earth Split in Two!' was the lobby-card headline, adding the subtitle, 'Today's Terrifying Look into What Might Happen Tomorrow!' Spectacular stuff, somewhat overlong, as cancer-ridden scientist and Nobel Prizewinner Dr Dana Andrews head up Project Innerspace. This international spot of cooperation has the intention of tunnelling down below to bring up some of the Earth's molten core and use it as an energy source. This is the molten Magma, stuff which when unleashed might well destroy our planet, or so warns handsome geologist Kieron Moore, a chap with his eye on the main chance and Janette Scott's legs, something he had caught sight of in the same company's sci-fi effort of the previous year, *The Day if the Triffids*. But cancer-ridden Dana cares not for the future, and clandestinely fires off an atomic missile into the fissure. This sets off the Crack in the World of the title, and the only answer is to explode an atomic bomb down the Krakatoa Volcano. It works, and gives the world a new moon, much appreciated by the young lovers.

ASTOUNDING ADVENTURE
FROM THE CENTER OF THE MOON
MUTINY IN OUTER SPACE
A WOOLNER BROS. Presentation starring WILLIAM LESLIE · DOLORES FAITH · PAMELA CURRAN · RICHARD GARLAND
and HAROLD LLOYD JR. featuring JAMES DOBSON Produced by HUGO GRIMALDI and ARTHUR C. PIERCE Directed by HUGO GRIMALDI Screenplay by ARTHUR C. PIERCE

# Mutiny in Outer Space

*Original title* Ammutinamento Nello Spazio
*1964* Woolner Brothers Pictures
*Distributors* Crest Pictures
*Producers* Hugo Grimaldi, Arthur C. Pierce
*Director* Hugo Grimaldi
*Screenplay* Arthur C. Pierce
*Camera* Arch Dalzell
*Editor* George White
*Art Director* Paul Sylos
*Music* Gordon Zahler
85 minutes

William Leslie *Towers*
Dolores Faith *Faith Montaine*
Pamela Curran *Connie*
Richard Garland *Col Cromwell*
Harold Lloyd Jr
James Dobson *Dr Hoffman*
Glenn Langan
Carl Crow *Webber*
Ron Stokes
Robert Palmer
Gabriel Curtis

This Italian/American co-production is set some years ahead, when the rotating Space Station X-7 is used as an international Earth-base for exploration of our planetary system. 'Astounding Adventure!' seems a pretty mild catchline for this sci-fi saga of creeping fungus, but it was all the lobby cards could offer. Astronaut Webber is the pioneering pilot who returns to SX-7 in his spaceship, infected with the stuff after exploring the ice caverns of the middle of the moon. He is the first man to grow fuzzy, a fiendish green, if we are to judge by the lobby card (which is in colour, of course, although the movie is monochrome). Dr Hoffman, the Space Station physician, contracts the fungus too, and realises, after a little self-experimentation, that it can be conquered with extremes of cold. Colonel Cromwell, however, in charge of operations, goes a bit barmy and refuses to contact Earth. This causes a rebellion on the Space Station. The mutineers refrigerate the place and radio Earth for assistance. Up comes a rescue squad, who bombard the buildings with frosted particles and freeze the fungus. Fifth on the cast-list lurks Harold Lloyd Junior: what would daddy say?

2
ALL-NEW THRILLERS
OF THE SPACE AGE!
Alan V. Iselin presents
FRANKENSTEIN
MEETS THE SPACE MONSTER
PLUS!
CURSE OF THE VOODOO
BLOOD SACRIFICE OF THE SIMBAZI!
JUNGLE TERROR!
NATIVE FURY!
RELEASED BY ALLIED ARTISTS

## Frankenstein Meets the Space Monster

*Also titled* Duel of the Space Monsters
*1965* Vernon-Seneca Productions
*Distributor* Allied Artists
*Executive Producer* Allen V. Iselin
*Producer* Robert McCarty
*Director* Robert Gaffney
*Story* John Rodenbeck, R.H.W. Dillard
*Screenplay* George Garrett
*Camera* Saul Midwall
*Editor* Laverna Keating

James Karen *Dr Adam Steele*
Nancy Marshall *Dr Karen Grant*
Robert Reilly *Col Frank Saunders*
Marilyn Hanold *Marcuzan*
Lou Cutell *Nadir*

A long, long way from Mary Wollstonecraft Shelley, or even from Boris Karloff, this catch-penny picture (shown on a double bill with *Curse of the Voodoo)* illustrates what happens when Princess Marcuzan (Marilyn Hanold) and her half-pint helpmeet, the aptly named Nadir (little Lou Cutell), come down to Earth. Their plot is to capture a little female breeding stock to take back to their dying planet. But along comes an android bearing the rather curious name of Colonel Frank Saunders. (These were the days before Finger Lickin' Chicken.) Princess Marcuzan promptly pulls her laser gun and zaps it at Frank's face. The result shows us the reason they called the film after Frankenstein. The aliens go on their way rounding up a woman or two, and Frank wanders about having trouble with his short circuits. Fortunately doctors Adam Steele and Karen Grant come along and render repairs so that Frank can have a grand finale fighting Mull the Mighty Monster. Once again the Earth is made safe for us Earthlings.

M-G-M PRESENTS
THE WILD, WILD, WILD PLANET
STARRING
TONY RUSSELL / LISA GASTONI
WITH
MASSIMO SERATO · CHARLES JUSTIN · FRANCO NERO · ENZO FIERMONTE
ORIGINAL SCREENPLAY BY
IVAN REINER
DIRECTED BY
ANTHONY DAWSON
PRODUCED BY
JOSEPH FRYD · ANTHONY MARGHERITI
IN EASTMANCOLOR

# *The Wild, Wild, Wild Planet*

*Original title* I Criminali Della Galassia
*1965* Mercury Films/Southern Cross
*Distributor* MGM
*Producers* Joseph Fryd,
Anthony Margheriti
*Director* Anthony Dawson,
(Antonio Margheriti)
*Story* Renato Moretti
*Screenplay* Ivan Reiner
*Camera* Richard Paliton
(Riccardo Pallattini)
*Art Director* Piero Poletto
*Editor* Angel Coly
*Music* Francesco Lavagnino
*Choreography* Archie Savage
85 (93) minutes Eastmancolor

Tony Russell *Mike Halstead*
Lisa Gastoni *Connie*
Massimo Serato *Nurmi*
Charles Justin (Carlo Giustini) *Ken*
Franco Nero *Jake*
Enzo Fiermonte *General*
Umbero Raho *Maitland*
Isarco Ravailoi *Hotel Agent*
Moha Tahi *Chief*
Freddy Under *De Lauty*
Lino Desmond *Schneider*
Franco Ressel *Francini*
Giuliano Raffaelli *Francini*
Victoria Ziny *Agent*
Kitty Swan *Agent*
Rosemarie Martin *Agent*
Rodolfo Lodi *Claridge*
Margherita Orovitz *Edith Halstead*
Vittorio Bonos *Dr Delfos (dwarf)*
Sandro Mondini *Dr Delfos*

This film began life in Italy as *I Criminali della Galassia*, which translates as *The Criminals of the Galaxy*. MGM, who released it to the English-speaking world, changed it to *The Wild, Wild Planet*. Then their lobby cards changed it to *The Wild, Wild, Wild Planet*. Meanwhile, director Antonio Margheriti changed his name to Anthony Dawson, but left it as Margheriti on the producer's credit. Not to be outdone, Carlo Giustini, actor, changed his name to Charles Justin, while as part of the plot, mad scientist Nurmi changed Dr Delfos (Sandro Mondini) into a dwarf (Vittorio Bonos). Finally MGM changed the running-time from 93 minutes to 85. Tony Russell, the star, didn't have to change his name as he had already done that during his previous Italian exploits in the historical superman style of thing (Hercules/Ursus/Maciste/etc). It is Tony who saves the sci-fi day, which occurs here around the year 2015, leading his lads against Serato's team of sexy supergirls, a bunch of rubberoid inflatables well-trained in karate.